Little Visits® Every Day

Little Visits® Library

Little Visits® Every Day

Little Visits® Library Volume 3

Mary Manz Simon
Illustrated by Beverly Warren

CPH.
SAINT LOUIS

Books by Mary Manz Simon

Hear Me Read Level 1 Series

What Next? • Follow That Star
Drip Drop • Row the Boat
Jibber Jabber • Rumble, Rumble
Hide the Baby • Who Will Help?
Toot! Toot! • Sit Down
Bing! • Come to Jesus
Whoops! • Too Tall, Too Small
Send a Baby • Hurry, Hurry!
A Silent Night • Where Is Jesus?

Hear Me Read Level 2 Series

The No-Go King • The First Christmas
Hurray for the Lord's Army • Through the Roof
The Hide-and-Seek Prince • A Walk on the Waves
Daniel and the Tattletales • Thank You, Jesus

Hear Me Read Big Book Series

What Next? • Who Will Help?
Drip Drop • Sit Down
Send a Baby • Too Tall, Too Small
Follow That Star • Where Is Jesus?

Little Visits® Series

Little Visits on the Go • Little Visits for Toddlers
Little Visits with Jesus • Little Visits Every Day

Stop! It's Christmas • God's Children Pray
My First Diary

Scripture quotations are from the Good News Bible, the Bible in TODAY'S ENGLISH VERSION. Copyright © American Bible Society, 1966, 1971, 1976. Used by permission.

Little Visits® is a registered trademark of Concordia Publishing House.
Little Visits® Every Day is an updated revision of the previously titled *More Little Visits® with Jesus* ©1988 Concordia Publishing House.

Copyright © 1988 Concordia Publishing House. Revised copyright © 1995.
3558 S. Jefferson Avenue, St. Louis, MO 63118-3968
Manufactured in the United States of America

3 4 5 6 7 8 9 10 11 12   06 05 04 03 02 01 00 99

.

For Hank—
1 Corinthians 13:4

Contents

Preface

"Why Did You Write *Little Visits with Jesus?*"

I've heard this question many times since the book was released in mid-1987. To be perfectly honest, I didn't want to write a book. As a mother of three young children and director of two preschool programs, there wasn't time to write a book. But our children weren't growing up with meaningful "Jesus times." That bothered me.

So I jotted down ideas on odd scraps of paper wherever I was: on attendance slips at school, napkins at fast-food restaurants, even bulletins in church. That's how *Little Visits with Jesus* happened.

And the response to it has been overwhelming. That's why you are holding *Little Visits Every Day*. Parents, grandparents, teachers, and Sunday school workers are seeking additional ways to share Christ with young children.

Devotions in both books are activity-oriented, child-centered, and organized for flexibility. *Little Visits Every Day* will work as a lap book for an adult to share with a younger child or for a child who already reads alone.

Substitute your child's name for those used in the devotions. This personalization will help your child become a part of the text.

Participate and interact with your child. You'll find natural opportunities to share your faith in Jesus Christ as Lord and Savior.

At home or in a classroom, pick a regular time for devotions. Don't worry about the number of minutes you spend. Any amount of time with Christ can be meaningful.

Then you will meet my hope for the *Little Visits with Jesus* and *Little Visits Every Day* books: that they help adults and children grow together as they grow to know Jesus.

May God richly bless all who participate in *Little Visits Every Day*.

MARY MANZ SIMON

Suggestions for Use

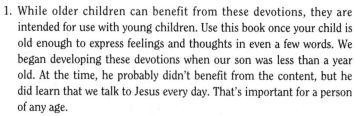

1. While older children can benefit from these devotions, they are intended for use with young children. Use this book once your child is old enough to express feelings and thoughts in even a few words. We began developing these devotions when our son was less than a year old. At the time, he probably didn't benefit from the content, but he did learn that we talk to Jesus every day. That's important for a person of any age.

2. Try to set aside one specific time each day for "Jesus time"—bedtime, before breakfast, after mid-morning snacks, etc. These very brief devotions will fit into almost any schedule.

3. Twenty-four devotions are provided for each month—approximately five or six per week. This allows you the freedom to extend a devotion into a second day, to create your own based on an important family event, or to consider Sunday worship at church as that day's "Jesus time." Also, because children mature rapidly at this age, repeating a devotion a month later will bring different responses and invite greater insights.

4. Whenever a devotion calls for responses, use whatever response your child offers to start a conversation, to extend your child's learning, or to clarify a meaning or feeling.

5. Scripture readings are listed at the top of the page, along with a pertinent excerpt. Whenever possible, read the selection from the Bible that belongs to your child. Or, as this book does, you might use Today's English Version (the *Good News Bible*) because of its simple language.

6. The devotions assume active adult participation along with your child's. When there are questions, talk about your responses as well as your child's. When an activity is suggested, participate with your child. In doing so, you, too, will grow in faith.

Little Visits® Every Day

There is nothing new in the whole world.
Ecclesiastes 1:9

Almost All New

Today we start a new calendar. It's time to talk about new things.

What is one piece of new clothing you have? What is something new at your house? Do you have something new growing in your mouth? Do you know a new baby?

There's one thing that isn't new this year. Jesus loves you. Jesus loves you in this new year just like Jesus loved you in the old year.

Even if you wear new clothes, have a new tooth, or even a new haircut—Jesus loves you.

Jesus' love isn't new. But Jesus' love is very, very wonderful.

Dear Jesus,
I'm glad I can start the new year knowing You love me.
Amen.

When they saw the child with His mother Mary,
they knelt down and worshiped Him.
Matthew 2:11

Christmas Isn't Over

Mei Ling was playing with the new clay she got for Christmas. Pretend you have some too.

Mei Ling was planning to make a scene of baby Jesus after Christmas. First she rolled and patted the pieces to make a little boy. Can you do that?

Then she made a round ball and pushed her thumb right into the middle. Mei Ling added a handle. There's a basket.

Now roll some tiny balls like Mei Ling. She is making toys to put into a basket for the little boy Jesus. Can you make something else with your pretend clay?

Sometimes we remember Jesus as a baby. But Jesus grew up. He was a little boy, then a big boy, and then what?

Yes, Jesus grew up to be our Savior.

Dear Jesus,

I'm glad You were born on the first Christmas. I'm glad You grew up to be my Savior. Amen.

When I look at the sky, which You have made ... .
Psalm 8:3

Glitter Angels

Michelle felt sad. All the Christmas decorations had been taken down. Everything had been sorted. Christmas was all boxed up in the attic. Michelle thought the house looked so bare. Now it was time for bed. Michelle was glad. It had been such a sad day.

But when she reached to pull down her window shade, she saw a beautiful sight. The back yard glittered in the moonlight. Snow, snow, beautiful snow. It was so sparkly, so Christmasy.

"Mommy, Mommy," Michelle called. "Come see."

Her mother stood with her at the window. Light snow was falling. But they could hardly see the flakes until they were on the ground. It looked like glitter.

"Michelle, I know you miss all the Christmas things," said Mommy. "And they are beautiful, but God sends many lovely things into this world for us to enjoy."

Michelle snuggled up to her mother. She felt so much better. Her mom was right. God did keep busy creating beautiful things. After all, tonight He even sent glitter angels to Michelle's back yard. And it was really gorgeous.

Dear Jesus,
Thank You for the beautiful things in this winter world. I especially like _____.
Amen.

Sing a new song to Him, ... and shout for joy!
Psalm 33:3

Loud and Soft

Make a loud noise with your feet. Now stop. What do you hear?

Make a loud noise with your hands. Now stop. What do you hear?

Make a loud noise with your hands and feet. Now stop. What do you hear?

Touch the part of your body you've been using the most. Did you touch your ears? your hands? your feet?

God has given us such wonderful bodies. Clap for Jesus! Now thank Jesus for you.

Dear Jesus,

Sometimes I forget to say thank You for me, the different parts of me that do all kinds of things. My hands can
_____. My feet can _____
_____. My ears can _____
_____. Thank You, God, for my body.
Amen.

*May God our Father and the Lord Jesus Christ
give you grace and peace.*
2 Thessalonians 1:2

Hi, There!

Instructions: Act out the answers to these questions with your child.

How do you say hello to someone on the telephone?

How do you say hello to someone who is across the street? (*Did you wave your hand?*)

How do you say hello when your relatives come to visit? (*Do you give a friendly hug?*)

How do you say hello to Jesus every day? Some children say hello to Jesus every morning when they wake up. Some children use the same prayer to talk to Jesus every day. Other children talk to Jesus as a good friend, using new words every day.

Tomorrow when you wake up, say hello to Jesus with your very own prayer. If you need help, ask an adult to pray with you. Jesus will hear you.

Dear Jesus,

Sometimes I get stuck after those words, "Dear Jesus." Help me remember You will listen to me even when I start my prayer with, "Hi, there, Jesus." You are my friend. You are my Savior. Amen.

*Kind words bring life, but cruel words
crush your spirit.*
Proverbs 15:4

Tongue Time

Instructions: Act out the devotion with your child.

Pretend to eat something salty. What do you like that's salty?

Pretend to eat something sweet. What do you like that's sweet?

Pretend to eat something sour. What tastes sour?

God made us with something very special to help us taste: a tongue. Wiggle your tongue. Our tongues are covered with taste buds. They don't look like buds on a flower. Our taste buds look like little bumps on our tongues.

The next time you eat something, remember your tongue and how it helps you taste. Then thank God for giving you a tongue to taste with. God has made so many wonderful parts of our bodies. Would you have thought to make a tongue that tastes?

Dear Jesus,

I don't often think about my tongue, my toenails, or other parts of me that don't seem so important like _____
_____. But those are all parts of me. Thank You, for making me me. Amen.

Your house will be my home as long as I live.
Psalm 23:6

Which Way?

Instructions: Help your child fill in the blanks.

I move down when I _____.

I go sideways when I _____.

I once walked under a _____.

I go backwards when _____.

I walk between _____.

I go underneath when _____.

Now here's a question: Which way will you go to heaven? That's a hard question because we don't know the real answer.

What we do know is that heaven is a wonderful place and Jesus will be waiting for us. Which way is heaven? "Toward Jesus" is a good answer.

Dear Jesus,

Sometimes I think heaven is _____

_____. I'm just glad You'll be with me there. Amen.

Be faithful to Me, ...
and I will give you life as your prize.
Revelation 2:10

The Saintly ABCs

Mrs. Dronen's class was having a great time. They were thinking of names of people in the Bible or of saints today that start with the different letters of the alphabet. Here's how their list started.

A—Aaron (Moses' brother)

B—Barnabas
   (look in Acts 13:1 to find out about this man)

C—Christ

D—Dorcas

E—Erin

"There's not an Erin in the Bible," said Tommy.

Z-Zacchaeus

"No, but I'm a saint because I know Jesus loves me," answered Erin.

See if you can finish the alphabet the class started. Remember to add your name when it comes to the first letter in your name!

Dear Jesus,

I know You love me. That makes me a saint. Help me act as You would like. Amen.

We are His people.
Psalm 100:3

Mr. Fix-It

Barry looked sadly at his teddy bear. The little boy next door had torn Teddy's arm almost completely off. Teddy was so special. It was Barry's very favorite bear. Daddy wouldn't have time to fix it until tomorrow. Poor Teddy. Poor Barry.

That night Barry prayed:

> Now I lay me down to sleep. I pray the Lord my
> soul to keep. When morning is breaking,
> Daddy'll fix it and Teddy. Amen.

When Barry's dad heard his prayer, he took Barry and poor Teddy in his arms. "I'll do my best to fix Teddy's arm, but I can't promise. Only God is Mr. Fix-It. He's the only one who can make everything right. I can only try my best," he said.

"God shouldn't have let Teddy get so hurt," said Barry.

"We don't understand everything that happens, Barry," said Dad. "But we do know that God always loves us. And tomorrow I'll have time to help Teddy."

"Thanks, Daddy," said Barry. "I'm glad God made you my daddy."

Who are people God gives to help you?

Dear Jesus,
    I don't like it when_____.
Sometimes I don't understand why things happen like
when _____. I do know You
always love me, though. I can always plan on that. Amen.

What Can You See?

It is 3 p.m. at Sarah's house. Let's listen to what she says to her dad.

"I think glasses will fall off my nose."

"Won't glasses melt next summer?"

"How will I sneeze with glasses?"

Now it is 5 p.m. at Sarah's house. Make your fingers into two rings and hold them around your eyes. Let's listen to Sarah now.

"I can see the raindrops."

"I can read that license plate."

"I never saw so many bird nests before."

What do you think happened to Sarah around 4 p.m.?

Dear Jesus,

Thank You for my eyes that see such wonderful things: pretty things like_____;

funny things like_____;

things that make me smile like_____.

Thank You for glasses that help some people see better like _____. Amen.

Hear my cry, O Lord.
Psalm 130:2

Sh! Be Very Quiet

Instructions: Act out the devotion with your child.

Don't use a single word now. Don't even open your mouth.

Tell someone you hurt your finger.

Tell someone you just got a birthday present.

Tell someone you lost a tooth—remember, don't open your mouth!

Sometimes it's hard to talk without words. But we can do many wonderful things without saying a single thing. Let's play again. No talking!

Tell someone you like them.

Tell someone you love them.

Now use some words.

Prayer suggestion: Talk to Jesus about what you did today.

It is time for you to turn to Me, your Lord.
Hosea 10:12

Time for Jesus

A clock tells us _____.

A kitchen timer tells us _____.

A watch tells us _____.

What is the same about a clock, a timer, and a watch? Did you guess that they all help us tell time?

What is one thing you did with your time today? What is one thing you did with your time during the night?

God gives us time for playing, eating, sleeping, and growing. He also asks us to use some moments for Jesus time.

Tomorrow, count how much of your day is Jesus time. You can use a watch to add up how many minutes you spend praying or telling somebody about God.

Dear Jesus,

Help me remember to plan some time for You every day. Amen.

Pray at all times.
1 Thessalonians 5:17

Jesus Time

Put your hand on your nose if you spent less than one minute praying to God today or telling someone about Him.

Put your hand on your baby toe if you spent more than one minute in "Jesus time."

Now fold your hands and put them in your lap.

Folding your hands in your lap is one way some people sit when they pray to God. That's a good way to have "Jesus time" every day. Some people stand up and tell friends about Jesus. That's another way to have "Jesus time." Some people are busy doing things to help others, to show love and caring. That's another way to have "Jesus time."

There are many ways to spend time talking to God or acting like He wants us to act.

Prayer suggestion: Spend a little "Jesus time" now praying to Him about your day.

*Let us run with determination
the race that lies before us.*
Hebrews 12:1

Gray Hair Talks

"Daddy says I gave you gray hair," Kelly told her mother. "I did not."

"What Daddy means is that I worry and fret when you disobey," said Mother. "People sometimes say a lot of worry can cause gray hairs to come more quickly than they might otherwise."

Kelly looked at her mother's hair. Some hair was gray. She climbed onto her mother's lap to look more closely.

"You mean this gray hair is because I cried when you wouldn't buy me gum?" Kelly asked. "And this gray hair is because I didn't pick up my toys this morning?"

"Well, sort of," Mother answered. "Maybe the gray hairs are talking to us."

Kelly listened. She didn't hear anything. "Maybe you need to work on being more obedient and following directions," Mother said. "Maybe I need to try to be more patient."

"Will that keep you from getting more gray hair?" Kelly asked.

"I don't know," replied Mother. "But it's sure worth a try. Let's pray to God and ask Him to help us."

Kelly asked Jesus to help her follow directions. Kelly's mother asked Jesus to give her patience.

When did you last pray with a grown-up?

Prayer suggestion: Ask the person reading this book with you to talk to Jesus with you now.

I call you friends.
John 15:15

Popsicle-Stick Pals

Lindsay looked sadly at her mother. The days in the hospital dragged so slowly. Lindsay had been in the hospital bed for a long time. She missed her house. Lindsay missed her dog, Snuggles. Most of all she missed her friends.

The only thing Lindsay liked was having Popsicles for dessert. And it wasn't even summertime! Her mom had been saving the Popsicle sticks. Now she had a big stack.

"We've got enough sticks today, Lindsay," said Mother. "Now we can make some Popsicle pals for you."

Mother got out some markers, glue, and little scraps of cloth. Lindsay watched her mom. First she drew a big black nose and some whiskers, and then she glued on two long pieces of brown cloth for ears.

"Snuggles," said Lindsay happily. "It almost looks like Snuggles."

Lindsay spent the afternoon making puppets of all her friends. She lined them up on the hospital tray. Most of the puppets were of friends in her neighborhood. There was one puppet, though, that didn't live nearby.

"This is Jesus, Mommy," Lindsay said. "I know Jesus is my most special friend."

Can you make craft-stick puppets of your friends?

Dear Jesus,
    You are my special friend. You are more than that—You are my Savior. Amen.

*Even the hairs of your head
have all been counted.*
Matthew 10:30

Growing Hair

Angie felt the top of her daddy's head. It was smooth. It looked very shiny.

"Daddy, the hair is gone from your head," said Angie.

"That's because I'm going bald," said Daddy.

"Well, how many pieces of hair do you have?" Angie asked.

"I don't know," Daddy answered. "Only God knows."

Angie felt her hair. It was thick and full.

"I'm not getting bald," Angie said. "I've got lots of hair. God would have to count a long time on my head."

"Oh no, Angie," Daddy laughed. "God already knows how many hairs you have. He knows all about you."

"Wow," said Angie. "He must be awfully smart."

Dear Jesus,

It makes me feel good that You know all about me. I know I am important to You. When I do things that aren't good, I don't like it that You know all about me. I know, though, that You'll forgive me. Amen.

This man really deserves Your help.
Luke 7:4

Helping Out

Holly was helping her dad. He had promised to give her a pack of gum if she would unpack groceries from the store.

She quickly gathered things for her dad to put in the refrigerator. What do you think she handed him?

Then she lined up frozen foods. What foods come frozen?

Now Holly stacked up canned goods. What foods come in cans?

At last Holly collected the boxes. What do you buy at the grocery store that comes in boxes?

"You've done a great job," said Dad. "Here's your gum."

Holly happily opened her reward. She was glad she had worked so hard.

We can't always get a present for doing work. Holly knows that. Several times she's asked a friend to come to church with her. Each time her friend has an excuse, even though she doesn't go to any church.

Holly is trying to be a good helper for Jesus. She's worked hard. But still her friend won't come. What would you suggest to Holly?

Dear Jesus,

I want to be a good helper for You. Sometimes that's easy like when _____. But sometimes that's hard. Help me remember to keep trying. Being Your helper makes me feel _____.
Amen.

We must thank God.
2 Thessalonians 1:3

Feet Are Neat

Instructions: Act out the italicized words with your child.

Here's a little game to act out.

A baby is sleeping; I must *tiptoe.*

I can *bounce* like a ball using my feet.

There goes a horse. I can *gallop* so well.

I like being a dancer, *twirling* around.

Marching in a parade would be fun.

I can *jump* like a kangaroo.

When skating, I *glide* back and forth.

I *walk* when I go into church.

Feet can do so many things. God certainly gave us neat feet!

Dear Jesus,

Thanks for feet. I especially like to walk to _____ _____. I run _____ _____. I jump _____.

Thanks for my neat feet. Amen.

He gave His only Son.
John 3:16

Song without Words

Where do you sing the song "Jesus Loves Me"? Althis sings it in the bathtub, especially in a bubble bath. Tamarcus sings "Jesus Loves Me" as he bounces a ball. Anne sings the song at church.

Amy sings the song at church, too, but she doesn't use words. No one can hear her sing. But you can *see* her sing "Jesus Loves Me." She uses her hands. She uses sign language.

Amy cannot speak using her mouth. She talks with her hands. But Amy knows where Jesus was born. Do you? Amy knows the names of some of the people in the Bible. Do you?

Amy knows what's important about Jesus. Do you? Now sing "Jesus Loves Me" with the person who is sharing this book with you.

Dear Jesus,
Help me use the words I know to tell other people about You as our Savior. Amen.

I have so much to tell you.
2 John 12

A Smiley Day

Look at this picture. Now make your face match the picture. Are you smiling?

This book was written so you could smile a lot. Jesus loves you, and that's worth smiling about. Jesus forgives you, and that's worth smiling about too.

Children who use these pages can smile because they know that Jesus loves them.

Smile! Jesus loves you.

Dear Jesus,

I can't smile all the time. Some things make me sad like _____. Some things worry me like _____. I get upset when _____. But underneath, I know I can smile my biggest smile ever because You are my Savior. Amen.

*Other sheep ... belong to Me that are not
in this sheep pen.*
John 10:16

Jesus around the World

Every night, just before bedtime, Chili and his dad sit down to read a book. The book has a picture on the cover. It shows some children reading together. Do you know what book Chili and his dad read?

Chili and his father read a copy of the same book you have. Children all over the world use this book. Maybe somewhere, another child is listening to this same story.

Where do you live? What language do you use most often? Where do you go to school?

Children who use *Little Visits Every Day* live in different countries, speak different languages, and go to different schools.

Chili and his dad read this book about 7:30 every night. When do you usually listen to *Little Visits Every Day?*

There are different ways to use this book, but one thing is always the same. Anyone who reads this book learns about Jesus. The same Jesus who loves you loves children in other countries too. The same Jesus who is your Savior died for children who speak many different languages.

Jesus hears prayers in many languages.

Prayer suggestion: Talk to Jesus about what is important to you right now.

Obey your leaders and follow their orders.
Hebrews 13:17

An Orange Tooth

This is a story about a child who lost a tooth. Have you lost any baby teeth yet? Do you know someone who has empty spaces in his mouth? Listen to Matthew's story.

"Matthew, did you brush your teeth?" Dad asked. Matthew nodded yes.

"Then why is that carrot sticking in your empty tooth space?" Dad asked.

"I thought carrots were good for me," said Matthew.

"Carrots are good for you, even your empty spaces," said Dad. "But that carrot just told me you didn't brush your teeth."

"I didn't know carrots could talk," Matthew said glumly.

"Now, go and brush your teeth," said Dad.

Dear Jesus,

Sometimes it's hard to tell the truth. Please help me remember it feels best inside when I'm honest. And I know You'll always forgive me when I say I'm sorry. Amen.

Every good gift and every perfect present comes from heaven.
James 1:17

A Cold Winter Day

Bang, bang, bang. Tyler could hear the hammering in the basement.

Clank, clank, clank. What could be making that noise?

The furnace was not working at Tyler's house. He wore a sweater, but he was still chilly. His feet were getting cold too. What would you do to keep warm at Tyler's house?

Klunk sounded some metal. What tool might have been dropped?

The house got colder. Tyler couldn't see his breath, though. It wasn't that cold inside. Finally, the furnace workers came upstairs. They were carrying their tools.

"You'll be warm soon," they said. "It's all fixed." Tyler was certainly glad to hear that. He was glad those people knew how to work with tools.

Has anything ever broken at your house? Who has fixed it?

Dear Jesus,

Thank You for giving us people who know how to take care of machines. Sometimes I don't even think of all the different things that could break down at my house. I'm glad machines keep working most of the time. Amen.

God ... decided that through Jesus Christ
He would make us His sons.
Ephesians 1:5

Being Adopted

It was snuggle time, just before bed. That was Pablo's favorite time.

"Mom, tell me again why I was 'dopted," said Pablo.

"We had lots and lots of love and nobody to share it with," said Mom. "We wanted somebody to love forever and ever. That's why we adopted you."

"Mom, tell me again why God 'dopted me," said Pablo.

"God adopted you as His child because He loves you too," said Mom.

"I like being 'dopted," said Pablo. "I like being 'dopted two times."

Do you know someone who was adopted once? twice?

Dear Jesus,

Thank You for adopting me as Your child. I know I am loved. I know You will always love me. Amen.

They will have all the bread they want.
Exodus 16:12

Bread Bits

Paige and her dad were shopping. The cart was almost full. "Run to the next aisle and pick up a loaf of bread, please," asked Dad.

Paige stretched as high as she could reach, but she still couldn't touch the bread. It was too high on the shelf.

"Daddy, I can't get it," Paige said. "The bread is too high up."

"That's okay," said Dad. "We'll get it down together."

"Daddy, if we lived when Moses was in the desert, we wouldn't have to reach so high for bread," Paige said. "We'd just have to look down on the ground."

Do you know why Paige said that? See if you can find the answer in Exodus 16:11–19.

Dear Jesus,

Thank You for giving me all kinds of breads. I like muffins, cakes, and especially cupcakes with _____ frosting. Crackers taste good with _____ _____. Thanks, Jesus, for breads. Amen.

The righteous will flourish.
Psalm 92:12

Birthday Blessings

Celebrating a birthday at church was such fun. Ryan's class would start singing "Happy Birthday." They would stop every time the word "you" came up. Then someone would tell one good thing about Ryan. He could hardly wait to hear what his friends would say.

"Happy birthday to you," the class sang. Megan said, "I like the way you shared the crayons with me today."

"Happy birthday to you," the class continued. Caleb said, "You walked to the bathroom with me."

"Happy birthday, dear Ryan, happy birthday to you," the class finished. Mr. Eggerding said, "Ryan, God has given you so many blessings. Let's thank God for bringing you to our church."

The next time someone has a birthday at your house or church, maybe you could sing the birthday blessings song. It's wonderful to see how good God is to us. What nice things will people say about you?

Dear Jesus,
On my next birthday, I will be _____.
I would like to _____.
Amen.

In this way you become My disciples.
John 15:8

My Way, Your Way

Jump in two different ways.

Now clap in two different ways.

Show you like someone in two different ways. Sometimes there isn't just one right way to do something.

People tie shoes in different ways. Can you show how to tie a shoe?

People pull out loose teeth in different ways. How do loose teeth come out of your mouth?

People also tell about Jesus in different ways. Some children invite their friends to church. Other children might take a Bible storybook to a friend who is sick.

There are many right ways to tell others about Jesus. Now think of two different ways to tell someone, "Jesus is your Savior."

Dear Jesus,

Help me try many ways of telling people about You. Amen.

43

When I go, you will not be left all alone.
John 14:18

So Far Away, So Near

It was another boring winter day at Ramon's house. He just sat looking out the window.

"Grandpa, why is Jesus so far away?" Ramon asked.

"Sometimes it might seem that Jesus isn't nearby," said Grandpa. "But sometimes Jesus is with us in the people who are near us."

"Ramon, who takes care of you when you are sick?" Grandpa asked. Ramon thought for a minute. Who takes care of you when you are sick?

"And Ramon, who makes you laugh?" Think with Ramon, who makes you laugh?

"Ramon, who makes sure you have clothes to keep you warm on these cold days?" Now you think about who cares for you.

"Jesus reaches out to you through people," said Grandpa. "So He's really not far away at all."

"And remember, Grandpa, Jesus is always with us when we pray," smiled Ramon.

Dear Jesus,

I know You are with me. You give me people who help me stay healthy like _____;
people who have fun with me in winter like _____
_____; even people I can send valentines to
like_____. Amen.

*The Lord God took some soil from the
ground and formed a man out of it.*
Genesis 2:7

Soft, Hard

Touch a part of your head that is hard. Next touch a part that is soft.

Now touch different parts of your body—one place that is hard and one place that is soft.

Here are some questions about hard and soft. What is soft that is inside you? What is hard that is inside your body?

God gave you a wonderful body. What do you eat that is hard? What do you eat that is soft?

One of the ways we take care of our bodies is to eat good food. What is your favorite soft food? What is your favorite hard food?

Soft and hard foods help our bodies grow. Before you eat next, thank God for the wonderful body He has given you. Then you can thank Him for the food.

Dear Jesus,

I don't think much about me, my body, that is. It's just here. I only think about it when something hurts or I need a Band-Aid. I'm glad I can use my body to do lots of things like _____ and _____.
Amen.

You did it for Me!
Matthew 25:40

Feed the Birds

Jacob's mother tugged at the heavy bag. Birdseed was heavy. She pulled and pulled. Finally she reached inside and scooped out some seeds. With a full bucket, she opened the door. The cold wind blew inside.

"Brr," said Jacob to no one at all. "No wonder Mommy wouldn't let me feed the birds with her today."

He watched from the window as his mother filled the feeder. Then she walked quickly back inside.

"Why do we have to feed the birds?" Jacob asked. "I thought it said in the Bible that God takes care of the birds."

"That's right," said Mother, "but one of the ways He cares for them is by having His helpers feed them. And we are Jesus' helpers."

"I know that," said Jacob. "I brought Cody to church, remember? And I pray every night. But I didn't know bird feeding was part of being Jesus' helper."

"It can be," said Mother. "Being a helper for Jesus can mean many different things."

How are you Jesus' helper?

Dear Jesus,

I try to be a good helper for You. One thing that's hard about being Your helper is _____.
I know You will always help me. Amen.

I gain wisdom from Your laws.
Psalm 119:104

A Church Museum

Kendra was tired of winter. But she wasn't bored today. She was making a church museum.

Kendra's grandma had found all kinds of scraps. Now Kendra was using them to make a display. Kendra was making one item from each of her favorite Bible stories.

First she made a little basket from an empty paper towel roll. (*Look in Exodus 2:3 to find the Bible story Kendra was thinking of.*)

Next Kendra got some foil from the kitchen. She made a crown. (*Check Matthew 2:1 to see where she got that idea.*)

Kendra needed a rubber band and a rock for the next display. She wanted to make a sling. Who used a sling in the Bible? (*Look in 1 Samuel 17:40.*)

Kendra worked all afternoon on her museum. Can you make a Bible museum too? What things would you make to display?

Dear Jesus,

I know the Bible is an important book. But it's also an interesting book. One of my favorite things in the Bible is _____. Amen.

My word is like the snow.
Isaiah 55:10

A Snow Dance

Instructions: Act out the italicized words with your child.

In some areas, February is a month with lots of snow. Act out the different ways snow can fall to earth.

Sometimes snow *floats gently*, like a feather.

Sometimes snow *blows in*, like a door that keeps banging.

Sometimes snowflakes *flutter*, one at a time, drifting.

Sometimes snow *falls heavily*, making a thick blanket.

But some things are always the same with snow. Snow is made of crystals. Snow falls when the temperature is cold. And snow is created by God.

Sometimes machines make imitation snow for skiing. Children sometimes use snow to make people and forts. But only God creates real, beautiful snow.

Dear Jesus,
    When the earth sleeps in winter, sometimes I forget some of the pretty things outside. Snow is pretty when
_____. Frost is pretty on the windows when _____.
Thank You for this winter world. Amen.

Be like newborn babies.
1 Peter 2:2

Babies

Brittany looked down at her baby sister. Since she had come home from the hospital, she hadn't done much. Cry and sleep. That's all Brittany's baby sister seemed to do.

"Why can't I touch her head?" Brittany asked her mommy.

"Lissa needs space for her bones to grow," said Mommy. "So she has a place on the top of her head that's still soft, with room for her head to grow."

Feel the top of your head with Brittany. Your head bones have grown together. Your head is hard on top.

"Why does she have a bald head?" Brittany asked.

"Hair has to grow too," answered Mommy.

Feel your hair with Brittany. What do you have inside your mouth that you can't see in a baby's mouth? Feel your fingernails. Are they hard? A baby's fingernails are often very soft.

"How will Lissa know to grow teeth?" Brittany asked. "And how will her fingernails get hard?"

"That's how God made us," replied Mommy. "Babies grow up in wonderful ways."

Think back to the last baby you saw. What do you remember about the baby?

Dear Jesus,

I can't remember much about being a baby. When I look at pictures of me as a baby, I see that _____ _____. Thank You for helping me grow. Growing up is _____. Amen.

Remember the miracles that God performed.
Psalm 105:5

All from a Tree

"Did God make everything?" Kara asked her mother.

Kara's mother looked up from reading the newspaper.

"Of course, honey," she said. "You know God made everything."

"Well, how did He make your newspaper?" Kara asked.

"Sometimes God works through people," explained her mother. "Pretend to make paper with me."

Act this out with Kara.

Chop down a tree.

Drag the tree out of the forest.

Chop the tree into tiny pieces.

Dump the pieces into a soft, gooey liquid.

Test the pieces now—they should be soft and sticky.

Roll the pieces so they flatten out like cookie dough.

Blow dry your thin piece of paper.

Cut it just the right size for a newspaper.

You're all done!

Dear Jesus,

I know God created the world. Sometimes it's just hard to understand how God created computers and spaceships and _____. Help me always want to learn more about You and our world. Amen.

God is love.
1 John 4:8

Tub Time

Robert was in the bathtub with his little brother. Robert was drawing valentines all over the tub walls with his finger and the soap. He wrote "Robert" in a valentine. Then he wrote the names of some of his school friends. Then Robert traced "Mom" and "Dad."

His little brother kept trying to make a heart. His finger always slipped when he came to the point of the valentine.

"I'll help you write somebody's name inside," said Robert. "That heart is good enough. Now, who loves you?"

"Grandma B. and Grandpa Hank," said John.

"Those names are too long," said Robert. "You made a little heart. I don't know if even a little name will fit."

Then Robert had an idea. He traced a cross inside his brother's tiny valentine.

"Do you know who that's for?" Robert asked.

"Jesus," said John. "Jesus loves me."

Dear Jesus,

Soap bubbles are such fun. I like to play in the tub. The water feels good, and I like to play with _____
_____. Thanks, Jesus, for a bathtub and soap. Amen.

You belong to God, my children.
1 John 4:4

Give Me Fives!

Instructions: Act out the devotion with your child.

Do these things with fives.

Hold up five fingers.

Touch five toes.

Jump five times.

Here are some thinking things with fives.

What are five things you know about Jesus?

Who are five people who go to church?

Who are five people you can invite to church?

Now clap five times for yourself. You did a good job!

Prayer suggestion: Talk to Jesus about how you feel right now.

Whoever loves is a child of God.
1 John 4:7

A Jesus Valentine

Demario was making a valentine to hang on the refrigerator.

First he got scissors. He would use them to _____ _____. Then he got some glue. He would _____. Next he selected some crayons. He would _____ _____.

Then he asked his mom for a picture. He looked through some old church papers to find just the right one. He found a picture of Jesus that would be just right.

Finally his valentine was done. It was ready to hang on the refrigerator in the kitchen.

Why do you think Demario made a Jesus valentine? Can you make one too?

Dear Jesus,

On Valentine's Day there are lots of heart shapes around. I know lots of people who love me, like _____ _____. I know that You love me as my Savior. Amen.

Whoever loves God must love his brother also.
1 John 4:21

Love, Love, Love

Instructions: Help your child fill in the blanks.
Here's a game to play about people you know.
My mom shows me love when _____
_____.

My aunt shows me love when _____
_____.

My friend shows me love when _____
_____.

Jesus shows me love when _____
_____.

Jesus doesn't give us hugs we can feel. Jesus doesn't kiss us or pat us on the back. But Jesus loves each of us very much. How does Jesus show He loves you?

Dear Jesus,
You give me people who love me like _____
_____. You give me people who have fun with me like _____. You give me people who make me laugh like _____
_____. Thank You most of all for loving me as my Savior. Amen.

See how much the Father has loved us!
1 John 3:1

Valentine Messages

Garrett sat quietly in the chair. His brother and sisters had come home from school with tons of valentines. Garrett had gotten three cards in the mail—one from his cousin and two from his grandparents.

"Nobody loves me," Garrett mumbled to himself.

His mom looked up. She had heard those unhappy words.

"Come here, honey," she said. "I love you, but I didn't send you a valentine card. I show my love for you in other ways."

How does an adult in your house give love messages?

"Your daddy loves you," Mother continued. "He didn't send you a valentine card." How do you think Garrett's father shows his love?

"Jesus loves you," said Mother. "I didn't see any valentines from heaven."

Garrett finally looked up. "I love you, Mommy," he said as he hugged her tightly.

"Just remember, there are many ways to say 'I love you,'" she said.

Dear Jesus,

I know You love me. You showed me that by being my Savior. Thank You for Your love that lasts all year long. Amen.

God ... has listened to my prayer.
Psalm 66:19

Have an "Ice" Day

Think of cold answers to these riddles.

A house made of ice is called an _____.

A bear that is the color of snow is a _____.

A bird that lives where it's cold is a _____.

One food I like that's cold is _____.

A way to get around on snow is by _____.

Life would be different if we lived where it's cold most of the year. It's probably cooler now than it is in summer.

What is something you wear now that you won't wear next summer? What is something you play now that you won't play next summer?

One thing will be the same, though. Whether it's hot or cold, Jesus is always ready to hear you pray.

Dear Jesus,

In winter I _____. In summer I _____. Winter and summer and all the times in between I know You will listen to me. Thanks, Jesus. Amen.

Love comes from God.
1 John 4:7

What Happens First?

Instructions: Act out the devotion with your child.

Before you cross a street, you _____ _____.

Before you eat hot soup, you _____ _____.

Before you go out in the rain, you _____ _____.

You probably put on your socks before you put on your shoes. You start to pump before you swing high.

Now here's something a little different: Before Jesus will love you, you don't have to do anything! Jesus will just love you. Nothing has to come before that.

Dear Jesus,

It's nice to know You love me, first, last, and always. Amen.

He spreads snow like a blanket.
Psalm 147:16

Snow Makers

Illita looked out the window. Another gloomy winter day. All green. No snow. There was never any snow. It was warm all year where Illita lived.

"Why can't we ever have snow?" Illita asked her grandma. "I'm tired of green, green everywhere."

Illita's grandma thought for a moment. She had seen snow when she was a little girl. What could she do for Illita?

"Let's plan a snow party," said Grandma. "You can invite some friends for tomorrow afternoon."

The next day, Illita and her friends had a wonderful snow party. They played with ice cubes outside in the warm sun. They had races to see which ice cubes melted the fastest.

Then they whipped up soap flakes with water. That made stiff "snow." They used this for snow pictures. Then they cleaned off the table with shaving cream—that felt like soft snow.

That night Illita gave her grandma a big hug. "Thanks, Grandma," she said. "The snow wasn't as good as God makes, but we had fun."

Can you be a snow maker at your house?

Dear Jesus,
Thank You for people who care about me like _____ _____. Amen.

The Lord is loving and merciful.
Psalm 145:8

Watch My Face!

Instructions: Act out the italicized words with your child.

Don't say a word now. Just show your feelings on your face.

When I think about Jesus loving me, I feel *happy*.
Sometimes I am *disappointed*.
Sometimes I am *afraid*,
But Jesus always *loves me*.
I *like* to talk to Jesus.
I tell Him *good things* that happen.
I *complain* about other things.
Sometimes I'm *upset*,
But Jesus always *listens*.
Jesus always *loves* me.

Dear Jesus,
Thank You for _____
_____ and _____ and
_____. I'm glad You are
my Savior. Amen.

Listen to my prayer, O Lord.
Psalm 102:1

I Want to Go Too

This was a sad bedtime. In the morning, Enrique's daddy would be leaving for a ski trip. Enrique wanted to go too.

When it was time for his dad's goodnight kiss, Enrique hid in his pillow. "It's not fair," Enrique cried. "I want to go too."

"Not this time," said Dad. "I really need a vacation just by myself. I need to get away. But you know I'll miss you."

"Grandma doesn't know how I like my bath all warm and bubbly," said Enrique.

"She can learn," said Dad.

"Grandma doesn't know I like cinnamon sugar on my oatmeal," Enrique said.

"You can tell her," said Dad.

"Grandma doesn't know how to pray my way," said Enrique.

"Oh, yes, she does," said Dad. "You pray like I do. And do you know who taught me to pray when I was a little boy? Your grandma."

Dad said, "Let's pray."

Dear Jesus,
    Please be with me
    As I sleep tonight.
    Let your angels guard me,
    Then send morning light. Amen.

A virgin will become pregnant and have a son.
Matthew 1:23

Remember Christmas?

"Grandpa, Grandpa," Ashley called. "It snowed last night. It looks like Christmas again."

Grandpa pulled open the drapes. It had snowed. It was still snowing.

"Can we get out the Christmas tree again?" Ashley asked.

"No, no," said Grandpa. "Let's just sit here and watch the snow. We can remember Christmas."

Ashley snuggled up to her grandfather. He felt warm and cuddly, just like Christmas.

"I know," said Ashley. "I'll pretend to do something Christmasy, and you can guess what I'm doing." Pretend with Ashley.

Reach forward to take a present. Now carefully pull off the bow and unwrap the paper. Open the lid. Show how you feel about your present.

Hand a present to someone. Watch as it's opened. Give the pretend person a hug.

Pretend to hold a book open in front of you. Sing your favorite Christmas song.

Ashley hugged her grandpa. "That was so much fun," she said. "It almost felt like Christmas again."

"It can feel like Christmas any time we remember Jesus' love for us," said Grandpa.

Dear Jesus,
    Thank You—again—for Christmas. Amen.

Let us go to the Lord's house.
Psalm 122:1

Sunday Stuff

Instructions: Act out the devotion with your child.

Stand up. We'll pretend that it's a Sunday morning.

Today is Sunday; let's pretend.
Get up; let's go. Now stretch and bend.
All ready now? Please walk and go.
It's time for church to start you know.
Open the door; step right in.
Sit down here; church'll begin.
Let's sing a song, then say a prayer
To feel God's presence. He is here.

Just one more song and church is done.
Stand up now for Sunday fun.
Reach out to greet and shake a hand
As people do across this land.
For Sunday is a special day.
It's time to rest, relax, and pray.

Dear Jesus,
    Keep me safe today
    As I laugh and run and play.
    May I remember You're with me
    In all I hear and do and see. Amen.

We love because God first loved us.
1 John 4:19

A Hero Forever

February is such a fun month, Chelsea thought. Every Friday night her family had an evening "with" a hero.

First they talked about a little brown animal. It would look out of a hole to see if there would be more winter. What was the hero that week?

The next Friday night, they saw a movie about a president who wore a big tall hat. He had a beard. Who was the hero that week?

Last week, they ate cherry pie. It was great learning about George Washington. Chelsea's dad had even pretended to be George Washington.

Now it was the last week of the month. They had to pick a hero for Friday night. Whom could they choose?

"Let's make Jesus our hero," Chelsea said. "But He's not a hero just for this Friday; He's always our Savior."

"We could have a little Christmas party," said her mother.

"We could bake Christmas cookies and sing carols," said Chelsea's brother.

"Then we could have something special for our hero of the week," said Chelsea. "But when we pray to Jesus everyday, we also know He's our Savior."

What do you think of that idea?

Dear Jesus,

You are special at Christmas. You are also special today on _____ (*day of the week*). You will always be my Savior. Amen.

Never forget what your mother taught you.
Proverbs 6:20

I Didn't Do It!

Grandma walked into the kitchen. She had just cleaned the floor, and it sparkled. Except for two big spills.

"Dawn and Wesley, come here," Grandma called.

"Dawn, did you make this spill?" Grandma asked.

"Oh, no, Grandma," said Dawn.

"Wesley, did you spill here?" Grandma asked.

"No, Grandma, I spilled over there," said Wesley. He pointed to the other spot. "I bumped my glass, and the juice just fell out."

"All right then, get a rag and clean it up," said Grandma. "So now we have a mystery. Who spilled here?"

What do you think happened? Who do you think will clean up the rest of the floor? Has anything like this ever happened to you?

Dear Jesus,

Sometimes it's hard to tell the truth. I'm afraid people will get mad at me. Please help me remember You will always forgive me when I make mistakes. Amen.

Jesus Christ is the same yesterday,
today, and forever.
Hebrews 13:8

Everything's Different

Nicole was tired of moving. Another new place to live. Another new place to find friends. Another new place to find a store for shopping and a park for playing. Moving to a new city wasn't any fun for Nicole.

Now it was Sunday morning. And there was something else that was new. Another new church! She liked the last house she lived in, her friends, her church. Nicole was very angry about moving again.

"I don't want to go to another new church," Nicole said. "There will be new kids, a new room, maybe new songs. I won't know anything."

Nicole's daddy listened. Then he lifted her up to his lap.

"Moving so often is hard," he said. "I don't like it either. But that's just the way it is now."

"I'm so tired of that lonely new feeling," Nicole complained. "Now everything will be different at this church."

"Not everything," said Daddy. "Jesus is the same. He's the same Jesus we prayed to before. He never changes."

When was the last time you saw a new person at church? What can you do to welcome the next new person you meet on Sunday?

Dear Jesus,
I think moving to a different city would be _____ _____. Help me be a friend for the next new person I meet. Amen.

65

God's word is good.
Hebrews 6:5

The Good Book

"André, please get me my Bible," said his grandpapa.

"Why do you read the Bible every day, Grandpapa?" André asked.

"I always learn something," answered Grandpapa. "Look, I'll teach you something. Here's the Bible. Now open it right to the center."

André took the Bible in his lap. He opened it up.

"See, you're in the book of Psalms," said his grandfather.

"Why does it say *John*, then?" André asked.

"What? Let me see that," Grandpapa said. He put on his glasses.

"Oh, André," he said. "This is just the New Testament."

"It looks like the Bible," said André.

"It is, but it's only part of it," explained Grandpapa. "When you open the whole Bible to the center, you find Psalms. When you open just the New Testament to the center, you find John."

His grandpapa chuckled and said, "You can barely read, but you sure taught me something about the Bible."

Try André's experiment. Take a Bible. Open it to the center. What did you find? Now take the New Testament. Open it to the middle. What did you find?

Dear Jesus,
Thank You for Your wonderful Book. Amen.

We love because God first loved us.
1 John 4:19

My Messages

If you want to send a message, you can mail a letter. Or you can give a message on the phone. How else can you give a message?

Let's play a message game without using words. Just act out these messages.

Be quiet!

That's scary!

I love you.

Jesus loves you.

Some children are afraid to tell their friends, "Jesus loves you." But you just gave that message without words. Next time you want to tell some-one about Jesus' love, you can use words. Or you can use actions. Those are both good ways to tell someone: Jesus loves you.

Dear Jesus,

Thank You for giving me lots of different ways to tell about Your love. The way I use most often is _____
_____. Amen.

Tools at Work

People use different kinds of tools when they work. See if you can think of two things that each of these workers use:

- a car mechanic
- an airplane pilot
- a nurse
- a helper for Jesus

Some of these jobs are just for adults. But adults and children can be helpers for Jesus. A helper for Jesus is called an evangelist. That means somebody who tells people about Jesus. You can be just as good an evangelist as an adult. Sometimes children are even better evangelists than adults!

You don't need a lot of tools to be a good helper for Jesus. You don't even need to go to school a long time. You can probably be a great evangelist for Jesus right now. It's an important job. And God has chosen you to work for Him.

Prayer suggestion: Talk to God about the work He has for you to do.

With my whole being I shall bring honor to Christ.
Philippians 1:20

Look at Me!

Instructions: Act out the devotion with your child.

Look at me! I can do this with my fingers.
Look at me! I can do this with my knees.
Look at me! I can do this with my ears.
Look at me! I can do this with my elbows.

There are many things you can do. But what is important is who you are. You can be kind and loving. You can be a caring person. You can be helpful. Most of all, you are a child of God. That's what makes you very, very special.

Dear Jesus,
Thank You for making me Your child. Amen.

The Spirit who is in you is ... powerful.
1 John 4:4

Singing Fun

"Frère Jacques" is a song you can sing as a round or a song to sing while clapping. Here are some new words for the tune.

Jesus loves me. Jesus loves me.
Yes, He does. Yes, He does.
Jesus is my Savior. Jesus is my Savior.
Yes, He is. Yes, He is.

I love Jesus. I love Jesus.
He's my Lord. He's my Lord.
He's my Lord and Savior. He's my Lord and Savior.
Yes, He is. Yes, He is.

Dear Jesus,

I like to sing about You. People sing about You a lot at Christmas, but I can sing about You anytime. That makes me feel _____. Amen.

He really is the Savior of the world.
John 4:42

Different and Alike

Instructions: Answer the questions with your child.

Here's something to play with the person who's sharing this book with you. Each of you can take turns filling in the blanks.

The city where you were born: _____

Your favorite food: _____

A smell you like: _____

The time you go to bed: _____

The name of a friend: _____

People are different in many ways. We're all the same, though, in at least one way: Jesus is our Savior. That's one thing that is important to every single person.

Dear Jesus,

My hair is a different color than _____ hair. I wear shoes that are different from _____ _____. I live on a different street than _____. But I know You love me and all my friends. Amen.

When I lie down, I go to sleep in peace.
Psalm 4:8

Night Noises

Reilly lay in bed. She was supposed to go to sleep, but she kept hearing noises.

"Mommy," called Reilly. "I hear a noise." Her mother came to the bedroom and listened. *Drip, drip,* they heard. Reilly's mother went to turn off the shower faucet.

"Mommy," Reilly called again. "I hear a noise." Her mother came to the bedroom door and listened. They could hear voices.

"I'll turn down the television," said Mommy. "Then you won't hear the commercials."

Reilly was quiet for a moment. Then she called her mother again. Her mother came to the bedroom door and listened. A motor rumbled.

"That's Mr. Moll leaving for work," Mommy said. "He's on the night shift."

"Mommy," Reilly called. "I hear … "

Her mother flicked on the bedroom light. The Bible was in her hand. She sat on Reilly's bed. She opened the Bible to a certain page.

"There are many noises at night," said her mother. "But this is what I want you to hear tonight. 'When I lie down, I go to sleep in peace.' Keep saying that to yourself, and you will get to sleep. Now good night."

What do you think Reilly did then?

Dear Jesus,
    Sometimes the night noises bother me like _____
_____. Help me remember You are with me. Amen.

There is no difference in the Lord's sight between one day and a thousand years.
2 Peter 3:8

Just a Minute, Please

One minute. Does that seem like a long time to you?

Ask someone to look at a clock for you. Now jump on two feet for one minute. Did one minute seem very long?

Now clap your hands for one minute. Did one minute seem long?

Wiggle your whole body for exactly one minute. Did that minute make you feel tired?

Jesus doesn't keep track of how long you spend with Him. He doesn't count the minutes you spend talking to Him. He's just always glad to listen to you.

Dear Jesus,

One minute seems like a long time when _____ _____. One minute seems short when _____. Thank You for the time You spend listening to me. Amen.

73

The winter is over.
Song of Songs 2:11

It's Still Winter

Has spring come to your house? Where Cory lives, spring should have started. The trees should be budding. The plants should be peeking out of the ground. But that's not happening. It's still winter.

"I'm so tired of winter," said Cory. "I just hate winter."

His grandpa heard Cory talking, and he smiled.

"I'm glad it's still winter," Grandpa said. "We haven't had our winter picnic yet."

"Winter picnic?" asked Cory. Then he remembered. Last year, they had a picnic on the living room floor. It had been fun!

"You make the sit-upons, and I'll pack the picnic basket," his grandfather said. Cory could almost taste the hot dogs.

He got busy with the sit-upons. First, he took two big paper bags and cut them apart. He and his grandpa would sit on those. Then he got out the crayons. He started drawing on the bags. Cory drew all the fun things about winter on his sit-upon. On his grandpa's sit-upon, he drew all about the best winter holiday, Jesus' birthday.

Cory and his grandfather had a great picnic. Afterwards, Cory decided he liked his sit-upon so much he'd hang it up in his room. What would you draw on your winter sit-upon?

Dear Jesus,
Thanks for winter. I almost forgot how much I like
_____. Amen.

[God will not] keep back His constant love from me.
Psalm 66:20

My Same Old Mommy

"Oh, your hair looks weird," said Angela. Her mommy had just come home. She had a new hairdo.

"What did you do to your hair?" Christy asked.

"Your hair looks funny," said Matthew. "Now you look like everybody else. I won't know you."

Mother said, "I'm still the same person. I just feel better with a new hairstyle."

All evening the children looked at their mommy. She really looked different than before.

But she cooked meatloaf the same way. She read *Little Visits Every Day* the same way. She even made them brush their teeth the same way.

Now it was time for bed. After Matthew and his mom had said prayers, Matthew said, "You look different with all those curls, but I know you're my mommy. You pray just the same as always."

Dear Jesus,

Sometimes people look different than I expect. That's hard for me to get used to. Help me remember that whenever someone or something changes in my life, You will always be the same. You will always listen to me. You will always be my Savior. Amen.

Guide me and lead me as You have promised.
Psalm 31:3

Leading Us All

Get ready to play a game about leaders. You can pretend to show different groups of people what to do.

Pretend to direct an orchestra. Take a baton in one hand. Ready? Be a conductor.

Think about being a drum major in a parade. Carefully balance that tall hat on your head. Ready? March.

Lead your own musical rhythm. Clap three times. Stamp three times. Have somebody copy your actions. Make up your own actions as a leader.

Many people are leaders. Some people only lead a group of musicians or people marching in a parade, but Jesus was a leader for us all. He showed everyone how to be a good Christian. He also leads us all to heaven to be with Him.

Dear Jesus,
Sometimes I am a leader when _____
_____. I am a follower when _____
_____. I can lead people to You by inviting my friends to church. I can follow You as my Savior. Amen.

For what is life? To me, it is Christ.
Philippians 1:21

Gone Forever

"I miss Mrs. Tullos," Caitlyn told her mother. "She always got me a birthday present."

"Mrs. Tullos died more than a year ago," said Mother.

"She's never coming back?" Caitlyn asked.

"No," said Mother. "That's what it means to die. You don't live on earth. You're in heaven with Jesus."

"I still miss her," said Caitlyn.

"Come here, honey," said Mother. "We can sit and talk about the good times you had with Mrs. Tullos."

Caitlyn and her mother sat and talked for a while. It was hard for Caitlyn to understand her friend was gone forever. But they remembered the Easter candy Mrs. Tullos had brought and the music box she had given Caitlyn for her birthday. Then Caitlyn and her mom talked about Mrs. Tullos being in heaven with Jesus. Caitlyn felt better, but she still missed her friend.

Do you remember someone who died?

Dear Jesus,

I'm glad people can live forever with You in heaven. Amen.

*You have trained children
and babies to offer perfect praise.*
Matthew 21:16

Counting Teeth

Juanita sat wiggling a tooth. It had been wiggly for a long time. Juanita thought she might help it get a bit looser.

"Mommy, did you lose all your baby teeth already?" Juanita asked.

"Oh, yes," laughed her mother, "a long time ago."

"Are you going to lose more teeth?" Juanita asked.

"I hope not," said Mom. "I try and take good care of my teeth."

"How many teeth do you have?" Juanita asked. Juanita counted her mother's teeth.

"Now you count my teeth," Juanita said to her mother.

"You have more teeth than I do," Juanita said when her mother finished.

"Teeth help us chew and talk and look pretty," said Mother. "I'm glad God gave me such good teeth. See how my teeth help me smile?"

Now look in a mirror. See if you can count your teeth by looking at your reflection.

Dear Jesus,

Thank You for teeth. I have _____ teeth. I know someone who has a loose tooth: _____ _____. I know someone who has a wiggly tooth: _____. I know someone who always brushes his teeth well: _____ _____. Amen.

He calmed the raging storm.
Psalm 107:29

Sleeping Upside Down

"Where are you?" Mother asked. She was coming to say good night to Ruai.

"Under here," Ruai said from under the covers. "I have to sleep upside down so the lightning won't come in my eyes."

"Oh, Ruai," Mother said. "Turn over so I can kiss you."

Ruai crawled out from under the lumpy bedcovers.

"There's a better way to handle a storm," said Mother. "Let me think a minute, and then we can pray.

When skies are dark and storm clouds gather,
You can sleep upside down,
But it's better now, to pray to God
Who'll be here all night long
To love you, keep you safe from harm

Until the morn-
ing light.

God is here, His
angels, too,

To watch you
through the night.
Amen."

Ruai looked up.
"Mommy, I love
you."

Dear Jesus,

Help me remember You will always hear my prayers. Amen.

Happy are the people whose God is the Lord!
Psalm 144:15

Smile Time

Smile a big smile. Frown a big frown. Make smiles or frowns as you finish each sentence.

I'm happy when _____.

I'm sad when _____.

I help others when _____.

Others frown when I_____.

I smile a lot when _____.

I'm sorry when_____.

There are smile times and frown times every day. When Jesus lived on earth, His life wasn't always wonderful either. But you can always smile when you remember that Jesus loves you. Jesus' love makes any time a smile time.

Dear Jesus,

Thank You for being my Savior. When I think of that, I can _____. Amen.

He is good to everyone.
Psalm 145:9

You Can't Buy Everything

Here's a thinking game. These are the easy questions.

What food comes out of a can?

What drink comes in a carton?

What food comes in a box?

Here are the hard questions.

Where can you get love?

What kind of a package does help come in?

Where do you shop for kind words?

Those are trick questions. You can't buy love, help, or kindness. We get those things from people. God gives us people to help us, love us, and show us kindness.

Before you talk to Jesus, think about people who care for you.

Dear Jesus,

Thank You for people who love me like _____ _____, who help me like _____ _____, who speak kindly to me like _____ _____. Amen.

Give us today the food we need.
Matthew 6:11

Heads, Bags, Bunches

Johanna and her mother were going to the store. Here is part of their shopping list. Part of the list ripped off. Can you fill in the blanks?

1 bunch of _____.
2 heads of _____.
1 bag of _____.
2 pounds of _____.

God's gift of food comes in many ways. Many families thank God for their food by praying at mealtimes.

When Johanna got home from the store, she made a place mat for each person in the family. She drew a picture of the person's favorite food. On each place mat she wrote, "Thank You, God."

Can you make place mats like Johanna's?

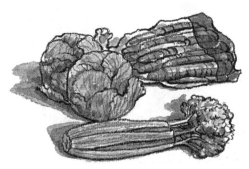

Dear Jesus,
Thank You for food that's crispy like _____
_____, crunchy like _____
_____, and soft like _____.
Amen.

Foxes have holes, and birds have nests.
Matthew 8:20

What a Trunk!

God made many wonderful animals. Some can do amazing things. But do you know what an elephant can do with just its trunk?

Stand like an elephant—you know how. Be sure your trunk is ready for some work. Swing it from side to side just to be sure. Now you're ready for action.

Pretend there's a tiger nearby. It's coming toward you. Now give a swing at the tiger with your trunk. God gave elephants powerful trunks full of muscles.

Now pretend you're hungry. Grab a bunch of leaves—just wrap your trunk around them and stuff those luscious leaves inside.

It's time for a swim. Get your trunk up like a snorkel. If you see danger, just go ahead and make a loud noise through your trunk.

Was that fun? God really made some amazing animals. But just think: God made us even more special.

Dear Jesus,

Sometimes I don't feel so special. But I am. It makes me feel special to know people love me like _____ _____. It makes me feel special to know You love me. And it makes me feel special to know You have a special job for me: to tell others about You. Thank You, Jesus. Amen.

Let us be brave.
Hebrews 4:16

Crisscross Fingers

Anne was trying to make an Easter card for her Aunt Ruth. She watched her big sister, Cary. Cary's card looked beautiful. Anne tried to copy it, but she couldn't.

"I can't do it," she said. She threw down her crayon. "My cross isn't even straight."

Anne's mom looked over to see what was wrong. She remembered when she was the little sister growing up. "Let me show you a trick," she said. "Your sister might not even know about this."

"Take your fingers and make a cross," Mother said. "I'll trace around them on your card."

"Neat," said Anne.

"Growing up isn't always easy," said Mother. "But remember you always have a cross with you. Problems won't go away, but you'll remember Jesus loves you."

"I love you, Mom," said Anne.

Dear Jesus,
   I like the way my fingers can make a cross. I'll remember that when I don't feel happy. You love me very much. Amen.

You show your care for the land.
Psalm 65:9

A Froggy Day

Jeremy opened one eye cautiously. It still seemed dark. But the clock said it was morning. Why was it like night? He could hear his father moving around in the kitchen. It must be time to get up.

He looked out the window. Everything was gray. Jeremy lived on the third floor of an apartment house, but he couldn't even see the street below. Then he knew. How would you describe the weather at Jeremy's house?

"Daddy, Daddy," cried Jeremy as he dashed to the kitchen. "It's all froggy outside. It's a froggy, froggy day."

His father turned toward him with a smile. "Yes, Jeremy," said Dad. "It is all gray outside. But the word is *foggy* not *froggy*."

"How did God do it, Dad? How did he make all the gray stuff outside?" Jeremy asked.

"Well, we know God didn't turn on a cloud machine," said Dad. "Fog is just a cloud on the ground. God controls the weather, but we aren't sure how. We just know He's in charge."

Jeremy spent most of the morning looking out the windows. The fog made everything different. Then the sun came out, and the fog was gone. Jeremy still liked his word *frog* better than *fog*, but he had a good day anyway.

Dear Jesus,

You are in charge of many different kinds of weather. My favorite weather is _____.
Amen.

God bless the king who comes
in the name of the Lord!
Luke 19:38

Parading Around

Let's have a parade. Forward, march! Kick your knees high. Swing your arms. Can you pretend to beat a drum? twirl a baton? play a big trombone?

When did you last see a parade? There's a story of a parade in the Bible. You can read all about it in Luke 19:32–38. You'll hear about a parade for Jesus.

Jesus didn't march like you just did. Jesus rode on a colt. If you had been watching the parade for Jesus, would you wave? call out, "Hi, Jesus"? clap your hands?

What did the people do in Jesus' parade?

Dear Jesus,

I think of You as my Savior, and that's good. Sometimes I forget You were a person too. You were even in a parade! Amen.

Sing for joy.
Psalm 67:4

Easter Carols

"Daddy, why don't we sing Easter carols?" asked Mari. "Like when we sing 'Silent Night' at Christmas."

"I guess you could call some of our Easter hymns Easter carols," Dad said. "Why don't you write a new song?"

Mari thought about that. She didn't know how to write very well. She didn't know anything about music.

"I'll help you," offered her dad. "Let's start with a tune you already know, like a nursery rhyme."

Her father wrote down some of the tunes Mari knew: "Row, Row, Row Your Boat"; "Are You Sleeping?"; and "Mary Had a Little Lamb." Then they thought about the Easter story. This is the new song they wrote to the tune of "Are You Sleeping?" Can you sing it?

Christ is risen. Christ is risen.
So we sing. So we sing.
Now it's time for Easter.
Now it's time for Easter.
Ding, ding, dong. Ding, ding, dong.

Work with someone and see what Easter carol you can write.

Dear Jesus,
　　When I sing, I feel _____.
I like to make my own music. I like to sing songs about You. Amen.

He is not here.
Matthew 28:6

An Easter Time Machine

Instructions: Act out the devotion with your child. You also can build your own time machine with empty boxes.

We're going back in time. Not back to tomorrow, not back to last week. We're going back hundreds of years to when Jesus lived. Ready? It's early on Easter Sunday.

First make a time machine out of pretend boxes. Don't forget to turn the wheels and dials to get back to Jesus' time. Now here we go.

It's Easter Sunday. You are up early in Joseph's garden.

Whom do you see first? What do you say? Act out the first Easter morning with the person who's reading you this book.

Here comes another person to the garden. Whom do you see now? How do you feel?

Finish up the story of Easter morning. It's almost time to climb into the time machine and get back home. Turn the dials. You're moving forward in time. Home at last!

Sometimes acting out what really happened can help you understand it better. Read the story of Easter morning in Matthew 28:1–7.

Dear Jesus,

Some of the parts of the Easter story are hard to understand. I know, though, You rose on Easter as my Savior. Amen.

Whoever believes that Jesus is the Messiah is a child of God.
1 John 5:1

Come Back, Friend

Jessica always felt shy around new people. Now here was a new girl at Sunday school. Should she smile at her? What would you do?

Jessica smiled shyly. The new girl smiled back.

When it was time to color, Jessica noticed the new girl colored almost as nicely as she colored. Jessica smiled at her again. The new girl smiled back. What would you do next?

Jessica said, "Hi, my name is Jessica." The new girl must be shy, too, thought Jessica. The new girl just said, "Hi."

Then it was time to sing. The new girl knew all the same songs about Jesus. What's a song you know about Jesus?

"Class," said Mrs. Randall. "We have a visitor with us today. Her name is Morning Bird."

Jessica looked at the new girl again. She had never had a friend named Morning Bird. But she hoped Morning Bird would come back to church. Jessica wanted to be friends with her.

What could Jessica do to help her new friend come back to church?

Dear Jesus,

Sometimes I don't know what to say to people. Help me remember that a smile or helping someone can show love. Thank You for showing love to me and my friends. Amen.

Whoever loves God must love his brother also.
1 John 4:21

A New Friend

All week Jessica thought about the new friend she had met at Sunday school. "Morning Bird, Morning Bird," the girl's name kept going around in Jessica's head. She hoped she would come back to church.

Jessica counted off the days of the week: Monday, Tuesday, Wednesday ... Finish counting the days until Sunday for Jessica.

Finally it was Sunday. And there was Morning Bird. Jessica skipped up the stairs to church.

"Oh, Morning Bird," Jessica said happily. She didn't feel shy today. "I'm glad you're here. I said your name all week. It's such a pretty name."

"It's Navajo," Morning Bird said shyly.

"Like an Indian?" Jessica asked. "But where are your beads and feathers?"

"Sometimes I wear a headband to keep my hair back. That has beads," said Morning Bird.

"I wear a headband sometimes too," Jessica said happily. "Let's hurry in. Will you be my friend?"

Jessica and Morning Bird sat next to each other all morning. They colored pictures together. They sang together. They prayed together to Jesus.

What are some things you like to do with your friends?

Dear Jesus,
Thank You for my friends like _____
_____. Thank You for being more than my friend. Thank You for being my Savior. Amen.

We have courage in God's presence.
1 John 5:14

Achoo!

Instructions: Act out the devotion with your child.

"Achoo," José said. "Excuse me."

"Achoo," José said again. "Excuse me."

"You've got quite a cold there," said Mr. Santiago.

"Achoo," José said. "It's not a cold. It's allergies. I sneeze like this all the time in spring. Achoo."

"What do you do about it?" Mr. Santiago asked.

"Achoo," said José. "Daddy gives me medicine sometimes, but it doesn't help much. Achoo. I just blow my nose a lot."

"That's too bad," said Mr. Santiago.

"Achoo," said José. "Achoo. Naw, it's not awful. I get to use different colored tissues. Achoo!"

Dear Jesus,

Thank You for giving me things to help me feel better like _____. Thank You for giving me people who care about me like _____ _____. Amen.

The Son of Man must be handed over to sinful men, be crucified, and three days later rise to life.
Luke 24:7

An Easter to Remember

"Well, Shannon," said Great-grandma, "come closer so I can see how you've grown."

Shannon moved a bit closer. Great-grandma's hair was white.

"And this couldn't be Shannon," Shannon heard someone say behind her. She turned around.

"Why, Shannon, look at you," said Aunt Meta. Shannon remembered her aunt's funny-looking clothes from last Easter.

"And who's this?" a voice said. Shannon turned again. It was Garrett, that cousin who teased her last year.

Shannon saw her mother moving into the kitchen. "Mommy," she whispered, "I want to go home."

"I know this might not be much fun for you," Mother whispered back. "But I don't see my family often, and I enjoy it. Here, take this."

Shannon moved to a quiet corner of the living room. It was a punch-out book about Easter. First, Shannon punched out a little cave; then she folded it together. Then she punched out a woman. Do you know who that might be? Then she punched out an angel. Where would Shannon put the angel?

Shannon felt much better just thinking about the first Easter day. Can you tell the story of Easter?

Dear Jesus,
The story of the first Easter makes me feel _____.
Thank You for being my Savior. Amen.

We want to do the right thing.
Hebrews 13:18

A Don't-and-Do Day

Waiting for Easter was hard for Kelly. She could hardly keep away from playing with all the Easter things.

"Don't touch the grass in that basket," her father warned.

"Don't play with the figures in the Resurrection diorama," Grandmother said.

"Don't stand in my light while I sew the hem of your dress," said Kelly's mother.

"Don't, don't, don't," said Kelly. "That's all I hear today. What can I do?"

"Do pick up these pins that I spilled, please," said Mother.

"Even when I can do something, it's work," Kelly complained.

"Kelly, there are things we must do and things we mustn't do in life," said Mother. "That's just the way it is."

"I'll bet Jesus didn't have rules when He was a little boy," Kelly said.

"Run and get the Bible, Kelly," said Grandmother. "Let me show you the rules Jesus had and that we still have."

You can find the same list of dos and don'ts in your Bible. Look in Exodus 20. What are some other rules around your house?

Dear Jesus,
Sometimes I don't want to do the things I should. Sometimes I want to do things I shouldn't. Please help me obey as Your child. Amen.

Jesus Christ is the same yesterday, today, and forever.
Hebrews 13:8

Antiques Are Old

"Now remember, Brittany, when we get to Aunt Sally's, don't touch the antiques," her mother said.

Brittany remembered the beautiful old egg from last Easter. It was tiny and painted—not a real egg, of course. But Sally couldn't touch it. The egg was very old. It was an antique.

Aunt Sally had a house full of old things. Brittany did not like some of the vases and jars, but others, like the egg, were beautiful.

"Are Aunt Sally's curtains antiques?" asked Brittany.

"No, they are just old," said Mother.

"Is Aunt Sally an antique?" asked Brittany.

"No," Mother said, "she's just old too."

Brittany was quiet for a moment. Aunt Sally's place even smelled old. It had a nice smell, a cozy smell, even if she couldn't touch anything there.

"Is Jesus an antique?" Brittany asked.

"No," laughed Mother. "Jesus will never get old."

Dear Jesus,

I like some things that are old like _____ _____. I like some things that are new like _____. I'm glad You're just always You. Amen.

You give them shelter from storms.
Isaiah 25:4

The Thunder Crashed

Instructions: You and your child can clap your hands each time the thunder crashes. Or give your child two pan lids to hit together.

Rain streamed down the windows. *The thunder crashed.* Trina did not like stormy days. This was definitely a stormy day. *The thunder crashed* again.

Trina ran to her grandmother. She was working at the sewing machine. *The thunder crashed.* Trina hugged her grandma tightly.

"I don't like the rain," Trina wailed.

Grandma put down her sewing. Lightning flashed across the sky. *The thunder crashed.*

"Stormy days might not be much fun for us," said Grandma. "But I always think of those little plants under the earth. If you go outside after the rain stops, we might even be able to hear them say 'gurgle, gurgle' as they drink in the rain."

Rain beat against the windows. It couldn't rain any harder. *The thunder crashed.*

"Rain, rain, go away," sang Trina quietly.

"Let's try a new song," said Grandmother. "Rain, rain, come and stay. Help the flowers grow today."

Trina looked up at her grandmother. *Thunder crashed* once more. "I still don't like storms," she whispered. "But maybe the rain will help the flowers grow."
Dear Jesus,

Help me remember You are with me, even when I am afraid. Amen.

He has been raised!
Mark 16:6

Spring Surprises

It's spring! Here are some spring surprises for you to finish.

A plant was starting to grow in Christy's back yard. Soon there was a bud. It wouldn't be long before something happened. Christy wasn't disappointed. Soon, a ____

_____.

Brian wanted to eat an Easter egg. First, he hit the egg on the edge of the table. Then he carefully peeled off bits of the shell. Inside _____.

Cole found a nest in the grass. It was almost covered by new green grass. He gently pulled back bits of gray and white hair. Inside was _____.

On the first Easter, a long time ago, a woman named Mary had a surprise. She was walking in a garden one day. To find out how she was surprised, ask someone to help you look in Mark 16:1–8.

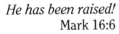

Dear Jesus,

The warmer weather is nice. The sky looks blue. Warm rains help plants grow. Spring is _____

_____. Amen.

The sparrows have built a nest.
Psalm 84:3

Building a Nest

Suddenly, there it was. A new nest. And sitting on top—do you know?

The nest really didn't appear like magic. It's just that Erin was seeing it for the first time.

First, the bird brought—can you guess? And then the bird probably looked for—what do you think? The bird needed something to hold together the twigs and sticks. What do you think she used?

But the bird nest might not have been a good fit. Show what you think the bird did now.

There. The nest is all ready. The bird is sitting on top of the nest. Oh—and look. There's something in the nest. Whisper—very quietly—what you think the bird is sitting on.

Dear Jesus,

My favorite spring bird is a _____
_____. In spring, I especially like it when birds _____
_____. Birds are one of the best parts of spring. Thanks, Jesus. Amen.

Come and see what the Lord has done.
Psalm 46:8

Spring Sayings

See if you can finish these sentences about the new season.

If the groundhog sees his shadow, _____ _____.

If March comes in like a lion, it goes out _____ _____.

April showers bring _____.

Just for fun, make up your own spring sayings.

A pussy willow says _____.

If you see a robin, that means _____ _____.

One thing we don't have to make up: Springtime means it's time to celebrate Easter. That's true every spring.

Finish these sentences.

Easter means that _____.

When I say, "Jesus is my Savior," I mean _____ _____.

The message of Easter is _____ _____.

Dear Jesus,

Spring means many nice things. Easter comes every year around this time. Thanks, Jesus, for Easter. Amen.

Why are you looking among the
dead for one who is alive?
Luke 24:5

Easter Cutouts

Trevor and Nicole looked at all the cookie cutters. The dough was almost rolled out. It was almost time to cut out the cookies. What cookie cutter would you pick?

Trevor took a bunny. Nicole took a baby chick cookie cutter. They started pressing the cutters into the flat dough.

"Be sure you make some cross cookies too," called their mother.

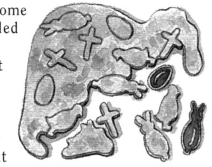

"But crosses aren't cute," Trevor called back.

"Oh, honey," said Mother. "We could have all the cute little cuddly chicks in the world, but that wouldn't make Easter."

Trevor and Nicole listened quietly.

"We could have furry little bunnies hopping all around, and that wouldn't make Easter either," continued Mother. "Put down your cookie cutters and let's talk about the real story of Easter."

Tell the adult who's sharing this book with you what happened on the first Easter.

Dear Jesus,

Bunnies and chicks are cute. I like the way bunnies _____ and chicks _____
_____. But I know You are the reason we have Easter. Amen.

I am going to prepare a place for you.
John 14:2

A Wonderful Day

Bethany was just lying in bed. She didn't want to get up. It was nice to lie awake and listen to the spring birds. Bethany just waited in bed, imagining the most wonderful day of all.

Pretend with Bethany. If you planned the most special day, what places would you visit? What people would be with you? What foods would you enjoy?

Tomorrow might be wonderful. But we know one time will be perfect: The days we spend in heaven. That's when everything will be great.

Do you know someone who is there now with Jesus?

Dear Jesus,

I like dreaming of special times. I know my dreams will all come true when I'm in heaven with You. Amen.

The Lord ... protects His people in times of trouble.
Nahum 1:7

A New House

Austin looked out the car window. There was his new house. It looked just like the picture his dad had shown him.

I don't want to move to another house, Austin thought. There was a little tree in front. It looked even smaller than in the picture. It would be a long time before he could climb that tree.

I don't want to move to another house, Austin thought.

The man who sold his dad the house pulled a key from his pocket. Austin and his dad stepped inside. The whole place was bare. There wasn't any furniture. There wasn't one picture on the walls. The windows were bare.

I don't want to move to this house, Austin thought. A tear rolled down his cheek.

Act out what you think happened next. Pretend to be Austin's dad. What will you say to your son?

Dear Jesus,
Some things seem sad like when _____ _____. Even when people try to cheer me up, sometimes I'm still sad. Help me, Jesus, to remember that You're always with me, You're always my friend, even in sad times. Amen.

*You soften the soil with showers
and cause the young plants to grow.*
Psalm 65:10

Spring Play

Instructions: Act out the devotion with your child.

All of these things happen in spring.

Buds open on trees.

It rains.

Children jump rope.

Bunnies hop.

It's Easter.

Birds build nests.

Worms wiggle through warm earth.

Spring is exciting. New things happen all the time outside. What do you like best about spring?

Dear Jesus,

Easter is one thing that comes in spring. Easter comes even if the weather is snowy or gloomy or stormy. Easter reminds me of Your love for me. Amen.

*All the people were amazed
at the mighty power of God.*
Luke 9:43

A Tummy Ache

Sarah rubbed her tummy. It hurt. She had a tummy ache. She lay down on the sofa.

"Daddy, my tummy feels off and on," said Sarah. She turned one way and then the other. She still felt odd. Sarah's father covered her up on the sofa. Sarah fell asleep. Her father called the doctor.

Did you ever feel like Sarah? Talk about what happened.

Dear Jesus,
I can help somebody who is sick by _____
_____. I know I can also pray that those who are sick get better. That helps too. Amen.

Christ gave His life for us.
1 John 3:16

Clues

"Mommy, did you and Daddy munch popcorn last night?" asked Matthew. He was looking at the living room sofa. Why do you think he asked that question?

"Amy, where did you put your muddy shoes?" Mother asked. She was looking at the kitchen floor. Why do you think she asked Amy that question?

"Why, Timothy, I'm glad you found your crayons," Dad said. He was looking at a piece of paper on the table. Why do you think he said this?

Sometimes people know about us by looking at clues. Matthew found popcorn on the sofa. That was a clue that his parents had eaten a snack. Amy left muddy tracks on the floor. That's how her mother knew she had been outside. Timothy colored a picture. That was a clue that he had found his lost crayons.

Now here's a situation for you to be a detective: How do people know you are Jesus' child? What clues do you give?

Dear Jesus,
I can give kisses. I can give a hug.
I can be caring as I share Your love. Amen.

He is a great King, ruling over all the world.
Psalm 47:2

Kings without Castles

Iola was waiting for a bedtime story. She was just learning to read so her mother always read to her. Iola was sitting with the Bible. It flopped open. K-i-n-g-s. "Kings," Iola read.

"Mommy, I read in the Bible," Iola called. "Kings, kings. That's what I can read. Is this all about kings?"

"Yes," smiled Mother, coming to sit next to her. "That book in the Bible tells all about different kings. Some did good things and some didn't do such good things."

Iola paged through the book of Kings. She looked up at her mother with a disappointed frown. "There aren't any pictures of castles and crowns," Iola said. "I like picture books."

"Well," said her mother, "sometimes in the Bible stories we have to draw pictures in our minds about what the words say."

"Sometimes I see pictures of Jesus with a crown like a king," said Iola.

"Jesus is the King of kings," said her mother. "After we read tonight, you can draw a picture of Jesus as the ruler of heaven. He's the King who always does the right thing."

Dear Jesus,

I know You aren't just a king with a castle, although I like to dream about castles and crowns sometimes. I know You are my Savior. Amen.

105

God will show me His constant love and faithfulness.
Psalm 57:3

Little Problems

"My toe itches," said Trent, "but only when I sit down."

"My hood falls off when I splash in puddles," said Nathan.

Sometimes little problems seem like big problems. Did you ever notice a secret about that? Little problems seem like big problems only when you're feeling grumpy.

It can help to look at things with a smile. You can look at big things, important things, then the little problems don't seem so big.

Here's an important thing: Spring is coming. Here's something else: Easter means Jesus is our Savior.

Here's another big thing: Somebody loves you. Somebody who lives with you, who gets you food, who kisses you good night. That's important.

Remembering the big things can help little problems go away. Try it!

Dear Jesus,
    I get grumpy when _____.
Help me remember the important things like _____
_____ and that You are my Savior.
Amen.

You are saved by the Gospel if you hold firmly to it.
1 Corinthians 15:2

Rainy-Day City

Rain was coming down again. But this would be a fun day anyway. Maria and her friends were making a rainy-day city. Yesterday, they had dragged home big empty boxes from a store. Today they were decorating their city.

Maria painted a sign that said "Groceries" on her box. What kind of store did she make?

Carrie brought a toy gas pump to set up in front of her box. What would she make?

Latoya carefully cut out pictures of flowers from a magazine. What would her store sell?

Jana carefully painted windows with pretty colors. She drew a cross. What building did she make for the rainy-day city?

"Let's make play money so we can go around and buy things," Latoya said.

"Nobody needs money for my place," said Jana. "Jesus is free."

Dear Jesus,
Thank You for giving me a church. Amen.

I Hear Spring

Grandma K. sat on the porch and smiled. Eric looked up at her and went on digging in the mud. Eric looked up again. Grandma K. was still smiling.

"Why are you smiling, Grandma?" Eric asked.

"I love the sounds of spring," Grandma said. "Listen."

Eric listened. A door banged. That was the neighbor's screen door closing. Do you hear any sounds of spring outside where you live?

Eric listened again. A motor started up. Soon Eric could smell newly cut grass. What motor did Eric hear?

He heard voices. With everyone's windows open, he could hear the neighbors talking. Can you hear neighbors' voices?

Eric looked at his grandmother. She was still smiling. "Grandma, you really like spring, don't you?" Eric asked.

"Oh, yes, Eric," Grandma answered. "And when I get to heaven, I'll feel as happy as if every day were a spring day just like this."

Eric thought for a moment. He didn't want to think of Grandma K. away from him in heaven with Jesus. But he remembered the smile on her face and knew she would be happy.

Dear Jesus,

I know heaven is a place where every day feels like spring. Thank You for the wonderful place You have waiting for us. Amen.

Whoever loves his brother lives in the light.
1 John 2:10

I'll Help You

Megan peeked into Amber's room. What a mess! Her sister would never get outside to play. Megan thought it would take a long time to clean up that room.

Megan ran outside. What a lovely spring day it was. Soon she heard her sister crying at the window. Amber looked sad.

Megan thought a moment, then ran inside. "I'll help," Megan said. "I didn't make the mess, but if we both work, it will get done faster."

Megan was showing love. What have you done recently that was caring? What could you do tomorrow?

Dear Jesus,

Sometimes it's easier to stay away from people who need help. You didn't, though, Jesus. Thank You for being my Savior. Help me be kind when _____ _____. Amen.

Look around you and see what is happening.
Isaiah 60:4

Play-Dough Play

Instructions: Pretend with your child to use play dough to make the things in this story by acting out the italicized words. Or use real Play-Doh or modeling clay.

Yukiko *rolled little tiny balls of play dough*. Then she *pushed her thumb into a big flat circle of play dough*.

"That's a bird's nest," said Kayla. "I'm making a spring thing too."

Kayla was busy making something that birds look for. She *rolled a long, long, very long piece of play dough*.

"A worm," said Yukiko.

Seth was busy making something for spring too. He took a big ball of play dough. He *pressed his thumb into the center until it made a big hole*. Seth stood the cave on the table.

Kayla couldn't guess what Seth had made. Yukiko did not know either.

"It's Jesus' tomb," said Seth.

"Oh, Seth," said Yukiko. "I could have guessed Jesus' cross, but you made something hard to guess."

What spring thing can you make out of play dough?
Dear Jesus,
Thank You for spring. Amen.

To the adult: Here's an easy recipe for play dough: Cook 1 cup salt, ½ cup flour, and 1 cup water over medium heat. When mixture is thick and rubbery, cool. Store in an airtight container. Dough will be less sticky after it cools.

Listen, Lord, to my prayer.
Psalm 86:6

How Do You Feel?

Complete these sentences. Whatever you say, your answers will be right.

When I get home from a toy store, I feel _____
_____.

When I leave the doctor's office, I feel _____
_____.

When I get home after playing in the park, I feel _____
_____.

When I leave church, I feel _____
_____.

We can have all different kinds of feelings. That's all right. Our feelings might even change. If you answer these same questions next week, you might give different answers.

It's good to know how you feel. Sometimes it's good to talk with someone about your feelings. Whom can you talk with about how you feel?

There is always someone who will listen to you: Jesus.

Dear Jesus,
　　Sometimes when I talk to You, I feel _____
_____. Sometimes I feel _____
_____. No matter how I feel, I know You will still love me. Knowing that makes me feel _____
_____. Amen.

Every three years his fleet would return, bringing
gold, silver, ivory, apes, and monkeys.
1 Kings 10:22

Animals, Animals

The zoo was a great place to visit. First Brandon and his mom saw an animal with a big, long trunk. The trunk went back and forth from side to side. Can you pretend to be that animal?

Then Brandon and his mom went to his favorite area. This was where animals were long and skinny. They slithered around or curled up, around and around. Can you be an animal like that?

As they were walking to the lion area, Brandon saw a beautiful bird, one he had never seen before. The bird had beautiful feathers, all spread out like a fan. The bird walked carefully. Brandon was afraid the big fan tail would make the bird top-heavy, but it walked so gracefully it did not fall. Act out how this bird walked.

"Mommy, that's a new bird," Brandon said.

"I thought you had seen a peacock before," said Mom. "It's not a new bird at all. Even King Solomon in the Bible had peacocks around his palace. Didn't God make peacocks beautiful?"

Dear Jesus,

Sometimes it seems like You lived long ago and far away from me. It's neat to think that there were peacocks and pigeons and eagles when you were a little child too. Amen.

My sheep listen to My voice.
John 10:27

A Good Shepherd

When Jesus was a little boy, some people worked as shepherds. Act out some of the things a shepherd might have done when

- a lamb got caught between some rocks;
- a sheep ate some fresh spring grass;
- a little lamb wanted to play;
- a lamb got lost.

Being a shepherd was a job with many different kinds of work. Did you know we have a shepherd too?

In the Bible, you can read about our shepherd, Jesus.

Prayer suggestion: Talk to Jesus about some of the ways He shows He is your Good Shepherd.

You provide the earth with crops.
Psalm 65:9

Touch Spring!

"Don't touch, Tricia," said Mother. She was holding a paintbrush.

"Don't touch, Tricia," said Grandfather. He was cleaning the lawn mower.

"Don't touch, Tricia," said Grandma. She was trimming the bushes.

There are many dangerous things lying around in spring. Some things help us do work but are not for children to use.

There are many wonderful spring things children can touch and enjoy.

Name something green you can touch.

Name something that moves outside that you can touch.

Name something else you can touch in spring.

Dear Jesus,

I can feel the spring air on my cheeks when _____
_____. I can feel the softness of spring when _____. I can feel the newness of spring when _____. I love spring. Thank You for spring. Amen.

They are a people whom I have blessed.
Isaiah 61:9

Who's Taller?

It had been a wonderful birthday party. Kristen liked her presents. She also liked playing with her cousins all afternoon. Just as everyone was getting ready to leave, Kristen noticed something. Her mother was taller than her grandmother.

"Mommy, will I be taller than you when I grow up?" Kristen wondered.

"Why, Kristen, I don't know," Mommy answered.

"Daddy, why are you shorter than Grandpa?" Kristen asked.

"Kristen, I don't know," said Daddy.

"Was Jesus taller than His father?" Kristen asked.

"Honey, we don't know," Grandma answered.

"Don't know, don't know," complained Kristen. "That's all I hear."

Grandma put her arm around Kristen. "It's been a long birthday," Grandma said. "It sounds like you're tired."

Daddy said, "I don't know why I'm shorter than Grandpa or why your mommy is taller than her own mother. But we do know that we love you no matter how tall we are. Jesus loves you too."

Look at some of your family pictures. Who is the tallest? Who is medium height?

Dear Jesus,
Sometimes I like to know all the answers. But You're the only One who really knows everything. Amen.

He gives orders to the winds and waves.
Luke 8:25

Blow, Wind, Blow

It's May! May is often a breezy month. See if you can make some wind. Take your hand. How can you make air move? Now blow on your hand. Can you feel the wind? Now stand up. Use your whole body to move air.

Air that moves is called wind. Wind helps scatter seeds so plants grow in new places. Wind helps dry up rain puddles. What else does the wind do?

We can't see wind, but we know when it's windy. Some people say the wind is like God. You can't see God, but you know He's there.

Look out the window now. Is the wind blowing? Perhaps the next time you see seeds blowing around or trees waving in the wind, you will be reminded of God. You can't see Him, but you know He's there.

Dear Jesus,
I know You're always with me. Amen.

*You have found out for yourselves
how kind the Lord is.*
1 Peter 2:3

Spring Cleaning

It was time for spring cleaning where Lauren lived. Lauren was to clean out her bedroom closet. But Lauren wasn't making much progress. She stopped to look at everything she found.

First she looked at all the gum wrappers thrown on the floor. Maybe there was a puzzle she had forgotten to play on the wrapper.

Then Lauren found an empty bottle of bubbles. She took that into the bathroom to fill with water. That would make a good vase for weeds she could pick.

Now Lauren found a puzzle she had forgotten about. This would be fun! She could work it right on the closet floor.

"Lauren," her father called. "How is your closet coming along?"

"Fine," Lauren called back. "My closet is still here."

What do you think happened next? You finish this story.

Dear Jesus,

Some things aren't much fun. I don't like to _____
_____. I don't like to _____
_____. Help me obey my parents and teachers, even when I have to do things that aren't fun. Amen.

In all things praise may be given to God.
1 Peter 4:11

Read All about It!

Kara couldn't wait to get to church. Last week, Miss Boyd had said, "We've tried to tell others about Jesus in many ways. You made invitations to Sunday school. You sent up balloons with Bible verses inside. Next Sunday, a newspaper photographer is coming to take a picture of your kites."

Kara and her friends had worked on their kites last Sunday. Each child had folded over the edge on a paper bag. Then the children punched two holes near the top edge of the bag. They glued long, pretty strips of tissue paper on the bag.

Today, Kara decorated her bag. She pulled yarn through the two holes. Then Kara and her friends pulled their Jesus kites outside.

The photographer had the children run back and forth in front of the church. Kara's paper-bag message was "Come to church." Other children had decorated their bags with "Jesus loves you" and "Jesus is our Savior."

Monday morning, Kara ran outside for the newspaper. The picture wasn't in it.

On Tuesday morning, Kara ran outside and picked up the newspaper. There was her picture! There was her Jesus kite! You could even read the words "Come to church" on her brown-bag kite.

Can you make a Jesus kit too?

Dear Jesus,
Help me keep thinking of new ways to tell people about You. Amen.

He gives a command to the earth.
Psalm 147:15

The Weatherman

The wind will blow;
Watch my hat go.
God's the Weatherman.

The sun shines bright
Until it's night.
God's the Weatherman.

The clouds fly high
Puffed in the sky.
God's the Weatherman.

The raindrops fall
So plants grow tall.
God's the Weatherman.

Give the weather report for your area today—the temperature, the sky conditions, and the wind.

Dear Jesus,
There are all kinds of weather. My favorite spring weather is _____

_____. Thanks for taking care of everything. Amen.

And so the word of God continued to spread.
Acts 6:7

A Grown-Up Party

Courtney's mother was getting ready for a party in the living room. But Courtney wasn't allowed to stay up late. She would be in bed.

"Why can't I stay up for the party?" Courtney asked.

"It's not really a party," said Mother. "It's just a talking party, really."

"No candles?" asked Courtney.

"No," said Mother.

"No presents?" asked Courtney.

"No," said Mother.

"Not even baseball-card trading?" asked Courtney.

"No," laughed Mother. "When adults get together, it's not always party time. We are going to talk about how we can invite more people to church."

"A church party?" asked Courtney.

"I guess you could call it that," answered Mother.

"If I think up some ideas for getting people to come to church, can I stay up late?" Courtney asked.

"We'll see," smiled Mother.

What ideas do you think Courtney suggested?

Dear Jesus,

I guess that being Your helper isn't always just fun. Sometimes it's work. Help me keep working, though, to tell other people about You. Amen.

Comfort My people.
Isaiah 40:1

A Bump on the Head

Bang.

"Ow, ow," cried Christy. "Mommy, I hit my head."

Christy ran to her mother. A bump had already risen on Christy's scalp. Quickly her mother put an ice bag on the bump. Christy's brother and sister stood and watched.

"Hold the ice bag," said Mother. "The swelling should start to go down."

Christy and her mom sat with the ice bag. Christy kept crying. Her brother and sister stood and watched.

"Silent night, holy night," someone sang softly.

"Who's singing a Christmas song?" asked Mother.

"Me," said Christy's little sister. " 'Silent Night' has such nice feelings. I thought it would help Christy's head feel better."

Sometimes it's hard to know how to help someone who is hurt. What do you do when a friend is hurt? Are there some things you shouldn't do when someone is hurt?

Dear Jesus,

Bumps and bruises happen when you're growing up like the time I _____. Thank You for people who help take care of me. Thank You for people who dry my tears like _____.
Amen.

Your word is a lamp to guide me.
Psalm 119:105

Boys in the Bible

"Grandma, come play with me," said Drew.

"Drew, you know I read the Bible every morning," answered Grandma.

"But I want you to come play with me," said Drew.

"Here," said Grandma. "You come play with me. We'll make a game of finding boys in the Bible."

"You mean kids are in there?" Drew asked.

"Sure," said Grandma. "Let's start by looking for a little boy who got a new coat." Use a Bible and look in Genesis 37:3. What color is your coat?

Now find a little boy who played a harp in 1 Samuel 16:23. Do you know any boys who play musical instruments?

Look in 2 Chronicles 24:1 to find the little boy who became a king. What would you like about being a king?

Drew and his grandma had great fun looking through the Bible. Drew learned the Bible is good for everyone. Do you know that too?

Dear Jesus,

Thank You for the Bible. I know it's for me, too, even with all the big words. My favorite part of the Bible is _____ _____. Amen.

May you be blessed by the Lord,
who made heaven and earth!
Psalm 115:15

God Made Everything

Midori looked sadly out the window. Rain was streaming down. She couldn't go out to play, even in the puddles. It was just too wet.

Midori did like to watch the bird outside, though. Rain didn't stop this robin. It stood on the grass and tilted its head to the side.

"What are you watching, Midori?" Mother asked.

"That robin is listening to the rain," said Midori. "Or maybe it's listening for a worm to wiggle around. But I don't see the bird's ears."

Midori's mother came to the window. "That robin is looking for worms," she said. "God put robins' eyes on the sides of their heads. The bird turns so it can see better."

"Wow, am I glad God put my eyes on straight," said Midori. "I'd get a stiff neck if I had to turn my head sideways to look for food all the time."

"Yes," laughed Midori's mother, "God made each of us just right."

jDear Jesus,
Thank You for eyes to see with. I like to look at _____
_____. Thank You for ears to hear with. I like to listen to _____.
Amen.

... the hour for prayer.
Acts 3:1

Ticktock

You can be a timekeeper. Pretend to be these different kinds of clocks and watches by making the sounds of the italicized words.

A grandfather clock goes *bong, bong, bong.*

A kitchen timer goes *rrrrrrring.*

A clock radio turns on with a voice giving the news.

A baseball-shaped clock goes *ticktock, ticktock.*

There are all sorts of ways to keep track of time. What other timekeepers can you think of?

The time you have today and the time you had yesterday are gifts from God. Sometimes we don't think of time that way. But God gives us time to use for lots of different things. What will you do with this next hour? You will have 60 minutes. Talk about how you will spend that time.

Dear Jesus,
    Thanks for time. Time to play _____
_____. Time to have fun with _____
_____. Time to pray. I want to tell You
_____. Thanks for taking
the time to listen. Amen.

Be quiet! ... Be still!
Mark 4:39

A Stormy Night

Crash went the thunder. *Boom* came the noise again.

The night-light flickered as the lightning flashed. It was a stormy night. Let's pretend you've just gone to bed. The storm outside is fierce. Act out what you would do.

Are you all snuggled down under your covers? Did you pretend to scamper to your parents' room? Did you pretend to cuddle up with a stuffed animal? Those are all things you might do during a storm.

Here's what Melissa did. She snuggled under her covers. She hugged her bear. Then she prayed.

Jesus, please stay near.
Help me not to fear
The lightning flash,
The thunder crash.
Jesus, please stay near.

Melissa felt much better after talking to Jesus. So she prayed again and again and again. Talking to Jesus is another good thing to do if you're afraid. Next time it storms where you are, talk to Jesus.

Dear Jesus,
Sometimes I get afraid when _____.
Help me remember I can always talk to You. You will always listen. Amen.

A child is born to us!
Isaiah 9:6

Picture Jesus

"Did Jesus really look like that?" Lori Ann asked her mother.

"That picture shows what one person thinks Jesus looked like," answered Mother.

"Was His hair that long?" Lori Ann asked.

"We really don't know for sure," Mother answered. "If you think of Jesus, do you think of Him with long hair?"

"Not as long as mine," said Lori Ann. "Did He wear clothes like that?"

"Honey, we really don't know," Mother replied. "We do know what's most important though—that Jesus is our Savior."

How do you see Jesus? Draw a picture showing how He looks to you.

Dear Jesus,

People have drawn lots of different pictures of You. Maybe Your clothes were _____.
You might have worn _____
on Your feet. I'm sure, though, that You love me. I'm sure You are my Savior. Amen.

Leave all your worries with Him,
because He cares for you.
1 Peter 5:7

Up on the Rooftop

Bam, bam, bam. Peter woke up with a start. What could be making that noise?

Tap, tap, tap. There it was again. What was that noise? Can you guess?

Peter peeked out the window. It was hardly even time to get up. There was a man walking on top of the garage. Then Peter remembered. Today was roof day.

Bam, bam, bam. Now he could see the worker making that noise. He was using a hammer.

Peter kept watching the worker. What a fun job! Then the man almost slipped. Peter didn't think it looked like fun anymore.

Peter tiptoed downstairs to his mommy's bedroom. "Mommy," he said quietly. "A man is hammering on the roof. Isn't he scared up there? Is Jesus watching him?"

"Peter, it sounds like you're worried about the roofer," Mom said. "Let's pray that God will protect him and give him a safe day."

Do you talk to Jesus when you're worried?

Prayer suggestion: Tell Jesus now about something that scares you.

The Lord worked with them.
Mark 16:20

Who Works Where?

Finish these riddles _____.
A banker works in a _____.
A carpenter works _____.
An archaeologist works _____.
A secretary works in an _____.
A bus driver works in a _____.
A Christian works _____.

There are many right answers for the last riddle. Christians are people who believe Jesus is their Savior. There are many Christians in the world. They work in all kinds of places. Christians can have two jobs at the same time. They can do their regular job, and they can do their job for Jesus.

Each of us has work to do for Jesus. If you are a good soccer player, ballet dancer, or bike rider, that's something you do well. But you can also be a helper for Jesus. Two jobs aren't too many when one job is for Jesus.

Prayer suggestion: Talk to Jesus about how you are a Christian worker.

All Scripture is inspired by God.
2 Timothy 3:16

God Is Love

Grandpa took off his glasses. He closed the Bible and smiled. "That's a great book," he said to Randy. Grandpa read from the Bible every day.

"I'm afraid of the Bible," said Randy. "It's so big and heavy."

"That's why you're growing big and strong," said Grandpa. Randy felt the muscles in his arms. Can you flex your muscles?

"But every page looks so crowded," said Randy. "It's so full of words that I'll never be able to read."

"Now, now," said Grandpa. "You come here." Grandpa flipped through the pages until he settled on one.

"Now you look here," Grandpa said. He pointed to three words in 1 John 4:8.

Randy read slowly, "God is love." Can you read those words in your Bible?

"But there aren't any pictures to look at," said Randy. "I like picture books."

"You think up pictures about the words," said Grandpa. "Now you think of a picture in your mind that says to you, 'God is love.' "

Think with Randy. What picture shows you that God is love?

Dear Jesus,

Help me grow up in lots of ways. Help me grow up so that I can learn more about You from the Bible. Amen.

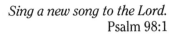

Sing a new song to the Lord.
Psalm 98:1

Old and New

What is one thing growing outside that is new? What is something growing outside that has grown there before?

Think of one thing you've recently learned to do or have done for the first time. Now what is one thing you've been doing a long time?

What's the oldest pair of shoes you have? The newest?

New things are fun. A new pair of shoes is sometimes squeaky clean. But after a while, even that lovely pair of shoes gets scuffed.

Jesus has been around for a long, long time. But as old as we get, we can still learn new things about Jesus. Talk to an adult about Jesus. Share one thing you know about Him. Then listen to an adult talk about Jesus. Can you each learn something new?

Dear Jesus,

Thank You for the excitement of new things—of people, places, and things to learn about and enjoy. Thank You for people who help me learn new things about You. Amen.

You created me.
Psalm 119:73

Movin' Muscles

We're going to do some moving around. Find a place where you'll be able to stretch and move your muscles. Ready?

Pretend to throw a ball. Now catch it.

Pretend to walk up the stairs.

Now reach for a sandwich. Take a bite.

In all these activities, you were using your muscles. Muscles pull one part of your body closer to another part of you.

Now show an adult what big muscles you are building: Bend your arm at the elbow. Ask the person to feel your arm between your elbow and shoulder. That muscle is your biceps.

Now use your muscles in another way. It's amazing how our muscles work. And God thought it all up. That's pretty special.

Dear Jesus,

When I draw, I use my muscles. When I jump, I use my muscles. I use my muscles when I _____
_____. Thanks, Jesus, for making my body work so well. Amen.

Then He gives a command, and the ice melts.
Psalm 147:18

Spring Things

The clouds are moving fast.
I hear the birds calling.
God is caring for me now.

Chickens are hatching.
Puppies are born.
God is caring for me now.

A neighbor plants flowers.
A farmer plants seeds.
God is caring for me now.

The warm winds blow.
Kites rise higher.
God is caring for me
now.

Dear Jesus,
    Thank You, Jesus, for giving us spring.
    Thank You, Jesus, is all I want to sing. Amen.

You make ... plants for man to use.
Psalm 104:14

Yum, Yum

A food that bakes before you eat it is _____

_____.

A food that pops before you eat it is _____

_____.

A food that boils before you eat it is _____

_____.

Before eating, many people thank God for their food. Our family holds hands while we pray. How do you pray before a meal?

We sing a prayer at our house. What do you do?

We use different prayers. What prayer do you say at mealtime?

People like many different foods. We even pray in different ways. But we pray to God and thank Him for what we eat. We can thank God for all kinds of yummy food.

Dear Jesus,

I like to eat _____. My favorite hot food is _____.
My favorite cold food is _____.
Thank You for yummy things to eat. Amen.

The Cemetery

"I don't want to go to the cemetery," said Chad. "It'll be boring."

"Mommy wants to see where her grandfather was buried," said Chad's dad. "That's why we're going."

"What's there to see anyway?" asked Chad.

"There will probably be a stone with his name on it," said Dad.

"I don't see how he can be buried in the ground and be in heaven with Jesus at the same time," Chad said.

"Only his bones are left in the box under the ground, Chad," said his older brother. "The rest of him is in heaven."

"Well, that's one way to look at it," said Dad.

At the cemetery, Chad's mother walked around to find her grandfather's place. The letters on the stone were so old Chad could hardly see them. Chad and his brother walked around the cemetery collecting pinecones. They laid the cones in the shape of a cross by the old stone.

Have you ever visited a cemetery? Some of the stones probably have crosses on them. Why do you think they look like that?

Dear Jesus,

Talking about a cemetery makes me feel _____ _____. Talking about being with You in heaven makes me feel _____.
Amen.

It is your own face that you see reflected in the water.
Proverbs 27:19

Making Puddles

Instructions: Act out the italicized words with your child.

Alka and Fumiko were playing outside. They were *carrying buckets* of water *to their mudholes.* Each one had dug a mudhole. And each mudhole was getting bigger. *Fill up the bucket, carry it to the mudhole, pour in the water. Fill up the bucket, carry it to the mudhole, pour in the water.*

"What are you making?" Alka asked.

"Mine is a puddle," said Fumiko. "What's yours?"

"Mine is a mirror," said Alka. "See, I can almost see my reflection. I can see the sun shining in my mudhole."

What would you do with your mudhole?

There are many wonderful ways to have fun outside. What ways have you had fun outdoors this spring?

Dear Jesus,

Sometimes grown-ups don't remember how much fun kid things are: like worms, and mud, and birds' nests. It's neat to think You might have played like I do when You were growing up. I'm glad You were a child once. I'm glad You are my Savior. Amen.

Go with God

Would you rather go to

- a birthday party or the beach?
- a swimming pool or a playground?
- a baseball game or an airport?

Summer is a great time to go many places. Everywhere you go this summer, you will go with God.

You may vacation miles away from your church, but God will be with you. You may visit people far away, but God will be with you. You may drive across town, but God will be there with you.

Dear Jesus,

My favorite place to go in summer is _____
_____. I'm glad You're always with me.
Amen.

Everything that happens in this world happens at the time God chooses.
Ecclesiastes 3:1

Pumpkin Flowers

Lisa loved to visit Aunt Sue on the farm. Earlier this year, they had planted pumpkins in the garden. Lisa couldn't wait to get to the pumpkin patch. Maybe we can have pumpkin pie for dessert, she thought happily.

Lisa and Aunt Sue walked through the garden. There were sticks holding up plants with big red balls. What was growing there? There were shorter plants with long green things hanging from them. What was that? Now Lisa walked to a big area with little hills and long green vines. There were big flowers too.

"Well, Lisa, how do you like our pumpkin patch?" asked Aunt Sue.

Lisa looked and looked. Do you think she saw any pumpkins?

"These are the pumpkin plants, Lisa," said Aunt Sue. "Pumpkins will grow on the stems here by the flowers."

Lisa was disappointed. There wouldn't be any pumpkin pie for supper tonight. "Why didn't God make pumpkins grow faster?" she asked.

"God has everything planned out, Lisa," her aunt laughed. "It would be pretty silly to see a jack-o-lantern in the summer. Besides, it would collapse quickly in this heat. Now our pumpkins can grow quickly with the warm sun."

Dear Jesus,

Sometimes I don't understand things. But I'm learning all the time. Something new I've learned is _____ _____. Help me learn more about You. Amen.

You created every part of me.
Psalm 139:13

Wiggles and Wiggles

"Why does your bunny wiggle its nose?" Amanda asked.

"Because God wanted Wiggles to be able to sniff the air all around," said Brock.

Amanda tried to make her nose move. Can you wiggle your nose? "See, God made me so I can move my nose too," said Amanda.

"Not the same way as bunnies," said Brock. "God made rabbits to wiggle just the tip of their nose. Then they can smell danger."

Amanda tried to wiggle her nose like Wiggles. Now you try to wiggle just the tip of your nose. Does it work?

"Well, maybe I can't wiggle just the tip of my nose," said Amanda. "But God let's me wiggle lots of other parts of me."

Wiggle something higher than your nose. Now wiggle a part of you that's lower than your nose. Now wiggle all around. Could a bunny do that?

Dear Jesus,

You made everything just right. I can do lots of things with my body. Thank You for giving me the ability to ____ _____. Amen.

*How happy are those who hear
the word of God and obey it!*
Luke 11:28

Churches, Churches Everywhere

Ashley loved to go riding with Aunt Hilda. She drove so fast things seemed to whiz by. At least it seemed that way to Ashley. Hospitals, schools, and churches all zoomed past the car window.

"Aunt Hilda, why are there so many churches?" Ashley asked.

"There are lots of places people can worship God," said Aunt Hilda.

"Are all churches religious?" Ashley asked.

"I'm not sure what you mean," said Aunt Hilda. "But around here, all the churches are places people go to sing and pray to God."

"There was a pretty one back there," said Ashley. "Why can't we go to the church with the big tower?"

"I like the way our church is," said Aunt Hilda. "I like the friends I get to see and how we pray to God."

What do you like about your church?

Dear Jesus,

Thank You for the chance to go to church. My favorite church song is _____.
Amen.

God created the universe.
Genesis 1:1

God's Creations

Instructions: Act out the italicized words with your child.

God created an animal that *crawls*. What did God create?

God created something that *blows in the wind*. What did God create?

God created something that *yawns*. What did God create?

God created you. What can you do?

Dear Jesus,

There are so many things I can do. I can crawl like a
_____, blow around like a
_____, yawn like a _____
_____. Help me remember one of the most important things I can do is tell other people You are the Savior. Amen.

God, may Your blessings be with us.
Psalm 90:17

Do You Sense Summer?

Is it summertime yet at your house? See if summer is here by using your five senses.

Can you smell summer? (*You might smell freshly cut grass.*)

Can you taste summer? (*You might eat fresh strawberries.*)

Can you hear summer? (*You might play outside with your friends and laugh and shout.*)

Can you see summer? (*Flowers might be blooming.*)

Can you feel summer? (*The sidewalk might be hot.*) Summer is one of the wonderful seasons God created so we can enjoy His world.

Prayer suggestion: Talk to Jesus now about some of the things you hope to do this summer.

I love the house where You live, O Lord.
Psalm 26:8

I Can Do It!

Instructions: Act out the devotion with your child.

You're bouncing a ball. You feel something drip on your head. There's another drop and another. Now you

_____.

You are jumping rope. Jump, jump, jump. You've been jumping for a long time. Your hand is tired of holding the rope. You _____.

You're swimming straight ahead. Splash! A big beach ball plunks down right in front of you. You _____

_____.

It's Saturday night and time to stop playing. "See you tomorrow," your friend waves.

"I can't play in the morning," you say. "I go to church."

Your friend says, "I never went to church."

You say, "_____."

Dear Jesus,

I do very well at a lot of things. With a ball, I can _____

_____. In the water, I can _____

_____. Help me to also be a good helper for You. Amen.

This is where the Temple of the Lord God will be.
1 Chronicles 22:1

Going to Church

Let's pretend it's Sunday morning. "Time for church" you hear someone call. Will you walk or ride to church? Act out how you will get to church.

Talk to the adult reading with you. Find out how your friend got to church as a child. When I was your age, I rode to church on a subway. That is a train that goes underground in a big city. I covered my ears because it was so noisy.

My mother rode to church too. When she was little, she rode on a streetcar that went down the middle of the streets. My great-grandmother didn't go to church. She was a pioneer woman, a homesteader. There wasn't a church where she lived. But she knew about Jesus. She read about Jesus in her Bible.

The next time you talk with an older person, find out how he got to church when he was younger. You might be surprised!

One thing won't surprise you, though. Even long ago, people learned about Jesus—the same Jesus you are learning about now. Jesus loved your mother or father the same way He loves you now.

Some things change during the years. But Jesus will always love you.

Dear Jesus,
Sometimes I like new things like when _____
_____. Sometimes when there's something different, I feel _____. I know You will always love and forgive me. Amen.

Children are a gift from the Lord.
Psalm 127:3

Who Is It?

Let's play a game with riddles about people you know. I will describe someone. Listen carefully. Your answers will all be right!

Someone you know has brown hair. This person is older than you are. Jesus loves this person. Who is it?

This person is younger than you are. This person still has baby teeth and can't do nearly as many things as you do. Jesus loves this person. Who is it?

This is someone who has lived a long time. You can tell this person is old just by looking at him or her. Jesus has loved this person for a long time. Who is it?

This child learns about Jesus in many ways. This child uses *Little Visits Every Day*. This child is growing up with Jesus. This child is looking at this book right now. Jesus loves this child. Who is it?

Dear Jesus,

Thank You for loving me and my friends: for someone who is older than me like _____;
for someone who is very old like _____;
for someone who is younger like _____
_____. I love You, too, Jesus. Amen.

The dogs under the table eat the children's leftovers!
Mark 7:28

Puppy Play

Mario loved to watch his puppy play. Cuddles would take the old towel and shake, shake, shake it. Then Cuddles would pounce on top of it, trying to pull it apart. And when Mario called, Cuddles would dash over to him, ready to play.

"Mario, I love to watch you play with Cuddles," said Grandfather. "That reminds me of your daddy playing with Tippy when he was a little boy."

"Have there always been dogs?" asked Mario.

"When Jesus was a little boy, a long time ago, we know that shepherds used dogs," explained Grandfather.

"Did Jesus have a puppy when He was little?" Mario asked.

"That I don't know," smiled Grandfather.

"Well," said Mario. "I'm just glad God made dogs."

Dear Jesus,
Animals can be such fun. My favorite animal is _____ _____. An animal can make me laugh when _____. Thank You for animals. Amen.

He gives food to every living creature.
Psalm 136:25

Picnic Time

What a beautiful day for a picnic, thought Yolanda. Each of her friends was bringing one thing for lunch. They would all eat at Yolanda's picnic table in the back yard. You can help plan the picnic.

Simone was bringing something to cover the table: _____.

Damian was bringing something to pour the drinks into: _____.

Jared was bringing cool drinks: _____.

Kim was bringing sandwiches: _____.

Stuart was bringing something for everyone to lay on their laps: _____.

Gregory was bringing fruit for dessert: _____.

Is there anything the children are forgetting?

The children arrived just around noon. It was fun to set the table. Yolanda's mother helped them.

"Before we eat," said Mother, "we always pray. Hold hands with the friend next to you. Bow your heads."

"I never prayed at a picnic before," said Simone.

"Picnics are something to especially thank God for," said Yolanda's mother. "Don't you think so?"

Dear Jesus,
Thank You for special meals like _____. Amen.

Anyone who gives you a drink of water ...
will certainly receive his reward.
Mark 9:41

I'm Thirsty

What would you drink

- that's orange: _____
- that's fizzy: _____
- that's good for you: _____
- that's from a faucet: _____

Now let's pretend. Take a glass full of your favorite drink on a hot summer day. Ready to enjoy? Drink slowly. Stop a moment to enjoy your drink. Wasn't that good?

Dear Jesus,
     In the summer, I drink lots of _____
_____. It tastes so_____.
Thanks for plenty to drink. Amen.

Love comes from God.
1 John 4:7

Read the Paper

Every Sunday after church, Emily's family sat down to look at the paper. Today, it was hot outside. It was hot inside. It was too hot to even read the newspaper. It was just a hot day.

"It's too hot to read," said Emily. "What can we do?"

Her father laid down the newspaper. He thought for a moment. "It's Sunday," he said. "Let's play a game with Sunday things. Emily, you go and get some crayons or markers for everybody."

"Now here are the parts of the paper you can use," said Dad. "Circle all the letters you can find that tell something about Jesus."

Emily and her sister Ashley looked through the pages. Emily found l-o-v-e right away. Ashley was just learning to spell. So Dad wrote some words for Jesus: Savior, Shepherd, Christ, Lord.

Soon the newspaper was full of circled letters. See if you can play this Sunday game. All you need is something to write with and an old newspaper. How many words can you find for Jesus?

Dear Jesus,
    I love You. Amen.

How great are your actions, Lord!
Psalm 92:5

Gifts from God

Here is a word game.

Something I ate today: _____.

Something I sat on: _____.

Something I played with: _____.

These are all gifts from God.

Someone I laughed with today: _____.

Someone I talked to today: _____.

Someone I played with today: _____.

These are all gifts from God.

We know God doesn't send us a bunch of bananas or a person to hug us right from heaven. But through people, He takes care of us. He gives us what we need. And through Jesus, we have the promise of living in heaven.

Dear Jesus,

Presents are fun to open. But I know every gift isn't wrapped in paper and tied with a bow. Thanks for today, even though things weren't wrapped up. Something I especially liked today was _____.
Amen.

There is no one like the Lord our God.
Psalm 113:5

All Fall Down

Justin carried his dinner plate to the sink. *Crash!* What do you think happened?

"It broke," Justin cried.

"That's all right," said Aunt Lisa. "Stand back so I can clean it up. I don't want you to get hurt."

"Why did it fall down?" asked Justin. "If the plate had gone up, I could have caught it."

Aunt Lisa laughed. "It fell down because of gravity. Everything pulls to the center of the earth. Everything pulls down," she said.

"Everything?" asked Justin.

"Everything," said Aunt Lisa. "That's why we don't bounce around when we walk."

"Who thought up gravity?" asked Justin. "I think that's a pretty smart idea."

What do you think Aunt Lisa answered?

Dear Jesus,

There are lots of neat things in this world like _____
_____. I know You must be awfully smart to think up everything. It makes me feel really special that You love me. Amen.

All night long the Lord protects me.
Psalm 3:5

Bedtime Already?

Devon lay in bed with her head propped up on her hands. It was still light outside, but her mother said it was bedtime.

Devon could still hear the neighbors outside playing. But her mother said it was bedtime.

Devon wanted to sneak out of bed and run outside into the summer night and play. But her mother said it was bedtime.

"Still awake?" Mother said as she tiptoed into the bedroom.

"It doesn't seem right that it's nighttime and still light outside," complained Devon.

"Summer nights are special," said Mother. "You can just lie in bed awake, thinking of the things that happened during the day. Pretty soon, it will be dark and you'll be asleep."

Think with Devon. What happened today that made you smile? What was something you did with someone else? What food did you really enjoy eating today? When did you show love or help someone?

Prayer suggestion: Tell Jesus about your summer day.

He listens to my prayers.
Psalm 116:1

The Longest Day

"Today is a special day," Mother said at breakfast. "This is the longest day of the year."

"The sun shines for more hours today than any other day," said Grandfather. "When I was a little boy, June 21 was always a day to do fun things."

"I'll serve something long for lunch," said Mother. What do you think they would eat?

After breakfast, the children went outside to play with something long. What do you think they used? Then they came in to have a long drink of cool water.

You can have fun on the longest day too. Measure who has the longest foot in your house. Whose arm is the longest? Look at a long book. Before you go to bed on the longest day, say an extra-long prayer to Jesus.

Dear Jesus,

I don't really think about how long the sun shines, just that it's up in the sky. Some days seem longer than others, but I know that's not just because of the sun. If I'm having fun, time goes fast! Thanks for keeping track of things so every year the longest day will always happen right when it's supposed to. Amen.

He has been good to us.
Psalm 118:27

A News Report

Pretend you are a television broadcaster. Give a love report from your house today.

Hello, and thank you for joining us at Good News TV. Here's what's happening.

A report from the youngest member of the family indicates this person was kind today when _____ _____.

A late bulletin from the oldest member of the household says love was shown when _____ _____.

Mother was so happy earlier today because _____ _____.

A good example of helping around the house was when ____ _____.

As we wrap up this broadcast, just a reminder from Good News TV: The best news is that Jesus Christ loves us all.

Thank you for joining us.
Tune in tomorrow for more Good News.

Dear Jesus,
It's good news at my house when _____ _____. I know sometimes the news isn't so good. That's when I remember that You forgive me. Amen.

The Lord remembers us.
Psalm 115:12

Pack Up!

"How is your packing coming along?" Nick's mother called.

Nick looked at his bed. He had piled up everything he could possibly need on vacation. What are five things you would pack in a suitcase for a vacation?

Nick went into his sister's room. A huge pile of things stood on the floor, waiting to be packed. How could a little baby need so much stuff, he wondered? What are five things a baby might need?

Then Nick went into his parents' room. A bulging suitcase stood at the door. A box of beach things was overflowing. What are five things adults might pack for a vacation?

"Wow," said Nick. "Do we have to pack everything?"

"Oh, not quite," said Mother, smiling. "We don't pack your dad, our baby, or … "

"… or me, or Jesus," Nick finished her sentence.

"Yes," Mother smiled. "Isn't it nice? Jesus always comes along with us."

Dear Jesus,
Thank You for coming along with me today when I went
_____ and when
I played _____. Amen.

Jesus got into one of the boats.
Luke 5:3

Goin' Fishin'

Martina was holding a pole with a string. At the end of the string was a little round ball. The ball was red and white. Martina sat quietly and watched the little ball. What do you think she was doing?

A long time ago, some people put out big nets in a lake. The nets felt light when they were empty. But pretty soon the nets got heavy. What do you think made the nets feel heavy?

People have fished for many years. How we fish today is a little different from how people fished long ago. But certain fish are still good to eat today, just as they were a long time ago.

Jesus lived near places where people fished. Some of his good friends were fishermen. You can read about Jesus and his friends in Luke 5:3–7.

Dear Jesus,

Sometimes I think things were very different when You were a little boy growing up. When I heard about You and Your fishermen friends, I felt _____
_____. Amen.

O Lord, You have always been.
Psalm 90:1

Lots of Questions

Sitting on Grandma's lap felt so nice and cozy. Rodong liked to sit here. But he didn't just sit. He always asked his grandma questions. Today was no different than before.

"Here come the questions," said Rodong, looking up at Grandma. "I've really been wondering about this. How did God get born?"

"Oh, Rodong," said Grandma, "That's an easy one. God always was."

"What do you mean?" Rodong asked.

"God has always been," explained Grandma. "He's God. He's been in charge of the world ever since He started it."

"So God must be very old," Rodong said.

"God is older than anything else in the world," answered Grandma. "Even older than me."

What questions do you have about God? Ask an adult to help you find the answers.

Dear Jesus,

Sometimes I wonder about things. I know I can talk to people like _____. Books have answers too. I know the book that has the most answers about You—the Bible. Amen.

... a leather bag full of water.
Genesis 21:14

All Wet

Instructions: Act out the devotion with your child.

Splash!

Swim!

Drink!

Wash your hair!

What did you pretend to use for each action? If you used real water, you'd be all wet. But we're just playing.

We use a lot of water. Water is such a wonderful gift from God. Think back—when did you last use water? Guess what you'll use water for next. When you do, say a quick thank You to God.

Dear Jesus,

My favorite thing to use water for is _____

_____. Amen.

I come to You for safety.
Psalm 57:1

Crashes and Flashes

Elizabeth sat up in bed. "Mommy, Mommy," she called. "Mommy, Mommy."

Her mother came racing into the bedroom. It was the middle of the night, but lightning brightened the whole room.

Elizabeth was crying. Thunder boomed. Elizabeth was afraid of the storm. Her mother held her close.

"Elizabeth," she said gently. "There's a wonderful little prayer you can say at times like this. I'll say it with you now, and we'll say it together the next time it storms. Then you'll know it by yourself."

Elizabeth snuggled closer to her mother. Her mother started to pray.

> When storm clouds gather
> And rains come hard,
> Jesus, be with me.
>
> When strong winds blow
> And skies are angry,
> Jesus, be with me.
>
> When thunder crashes
> And lightning flashes,
> Jesus, be with me.

The next time it stormed, Elizabeth went to her mother again. They prayed together. Can you use this prayer when it storms at your house?

Dear Jesus,
> After rain falls
> When skies clear,
> Jesus, be with me. Amen.

You will remain.
Hebrews 1:11

Changes, Changes

If you drop a slice of bread into a toaster, the bread will change to _____.

If waves bump into a sand castle, the castle will _____ _____.

If you pour batter into a cake pan and bake it in the oven, the batter will _____.

Many things change. Some changes are good. Some changes are not so good. Even you change. Think back to last summer. How were you different last June?

Many things change, but Jesus never does. He is our friend. He will always be our friend. Jesus is our Savior. He will always be our Savior. He loves us today. Jesus will always love us. Jesus never changes.

Dear Jesus,

Sometimes changes are fun, like when a cocoon changes into a _____. Other changes aren't so nice, like when a friend has to move or when _____. Thank You for always being You and staying with me. Amen.

The Lord guides a man in the way he should go.
Psalm 37:23

All Kinds of Work

Try some hand work: Touch your elbow to your little finger.

Try some foot work: Walk on your heels.

Try some head work: How can you tell a clock is running?

Heart work is special work. That's how we are Jesus' helpers. You've done hand work, foot work, and head work. Now answer this: How can you do heart work?

Dear Jesus,

Some things are easy like _____
_____. Some things are hard for me like _____
_____. Working for You is _____
_____. Amen.

Give us day by day the food we need.
Luke 11:3

Feeding Time at the Zoo

"Time to eat," Dad called as everyone trooped by the lion's cage.

"Now what do you want?" he asked. The children were all sitting at a picnic bench. What would you order for lunch at the zoo?

"I'm a hamburger person," Sarah said. What would you eat with a hamburger?

"I'm a hot dog person," said Kristin. What do you like on a hot dog?

"I'm just me, and I don't know what to eat," said Kali. What would you suggest to Kali?

There are many wonderful foods. Before these people ate lunch at the zoo, they said thank You to God. What prayer do you say before you eat?

Dear Jesus,

Thank You for all the wonderful things we can eat. I especially like a lunch of _____.
Amen.

He spreads clouds over the sky.
Psalm 147:8

Look Up!

Instructions: Act out the devotion with your child.

It was such a lazy day. Paige and Cole were just lying on their backs watching the clouds. They didn't feel like playing anything. Then Paige said, "Let's do 'What Flies?' "

Paige got up and ran around. She held her arms straight out from her sides. "Zoom, zoom," she said, running around. What was Paige pretending to be?

"That's easy," said Cole. "You're a jet plane. Now watch me." Cole got way down to the ground. He counted down, starting with 10. When he got to 1, he yelled, "Blast off." What was he pretending to be?

"That's easy," said Paige. "You were a rocket ship. Now, watch me." Paige ran around on tiptoes, flapping her wings gently. She sang a church song. What was she pretending to be?

Paige was playing angel. We haven't seen angels fly. But you can read in the Bible what we know about angels.

Dear Jesus,

I like to hear about angels. I know You send angels to protect me. I think angels are _____
_____. Amen.

Countless creatures live.
Psalm 104:25

Turtle Talk

"Look what we found," Courtney shouted. "Come and see."

Jason ran quickly. Courtney was pointing to a place in the grass. There was an ugly looking creature, Jason thought. It looked like a round rock with four little feet sticking out and a short neck. As soon as Jason moved closer, in went the head. In went the legs. What had Courtney found?

"Ah, now you scared my turtle," Courtney said.

"Who wants an old turtle anyway?" said Jason. "I've got Petey, and he's a great pet."

"My turtle doesn't like you," said Courtney. "It smelled you coming and went in its house."

"Smelled me?" Jason asked. "Turtles can smell?"

"Sure," said Courtney. "Don't you know anything? Turtles can't hear very well, and they don't have teeth, but they can sure smell."

"Well, so what?" said Jason.

"I'm going snail hunting," said Courtney. "Box turtles love to eat them. Turtles are pretty neat. Didn't you know God made some really great animals?"

"Sure," said Jason. "He made Petey, my salamander."

What animals do you like?

Dear Jesus,

I live in a wonderful world. It's filled with so many of Your creations. Thanks for animals I see at the zoo like _____and creatures I can find right near where I live like _____.
Amen.

You make ... plants for man to use.
Psalm 104:14

Slurp!

"Jeremiah, don't slurp," said Aunt Elise.

"But this is the only way I can eat," Jeremiah said. This was his favorite summer food—the cool, wet taste he loved so much. Having seed-spitting contests with his cousins was second best.

He'd watched the vines grow in the field. Then Jeremiah had watched the melons grow—from little to, oh, so big. What do you think Jeremiah was eating?

"How does a watermelon get black and white seeds?" Jeremiah's little brother asked.

"The water in the melon makes the seeds grow," explained his cousin.

"Are you kidding?" Jeremiah asked. "Don't you know anything? That's not right. God just makes watermelons that way. That's it."

Aunt Elise couldn't help smiling. Jeremiah was right. God planned such a wonderful world, she thought, even watermelons have seeds that are fun and colorful.

Dear Jesus,

Thank You for the foods of summer. I especially like
_____. Amen.

Your word is a lamp to guide me.
Psalm 119:105

Meet a Reporter

Sometimes in my job, I am a reporter. I learn a lot about something so I can write a story. Usually I ask questions. Let's pretend you're getting ready to report a story.

You'll need something to write with. What would you use?

You'll need something to write on. What would you take along?

Can you think of anything else you'll need on the job?

Here's your assignment. You are to find out all you can about what happened when Jesus was with the little children. Look in Matthew 19:13–15. Ask someone to read it to you. What can you report about that event?

Dear Jesus,
Thank You for the Bible that tells us about Your life. Amen.

The Lord provides for those He loves,
while they are asleep.
Psalm 127:2

Good Night

Demetrius looked up as his dad walked by his bedroom door. "Still not asleep?" Dad asked.

"No, I like night," said Demetrius. "It's so cozy, and I can hear lots of things I can't hear in the daytime."

Demetrius slid over as his dad sat down on the bed. What nighttime noises do you think he heard?

"Some nights I lie here a long time before I fall asleep," said Demetrius. "I like to guess what makes the different shadows." What makes shadows on your bedroom walls?

"Some nights I don't do that," said Demetrius. "Some nights I just talk to Jesus.

"I don't pray," explained Demetrius. "I just talk to Jesus. I like to tell Him what I did, what I played, what went wrong. Those kinds of things."

"That's a wonderful way to end your day," said Dad. "Just you and Jesus."

Dear Jesus,

Help me remember I can always talk with You even if my words don't sound like a prayer. Amen.

To have good fruit you must have a healthy tree.
Matthew 12:33

Trees

Instructions: Help your child fill in the blanks.

A tree can be a place for me to _____.

A tree is where birds can _____.

In a tree, a squirrel can _____.

On a hot summer day, a tree _____.

A forest full of trees _____.

My favorite thing about trees is _____.

Dear Jesus,
    Thanks for trees. Amen.

It is sung by children and babies.
Psalm 8:2

Play Ball!

See if you know about these different balls.

You hit this ball with a bat. The ball is a _____ _____.

You throw this ball into a hoop. The ball is a _____ _____.

You kick this ball into a net. The ball is a _____ _____.

You throw and kick this ball to win the game. The ball is a _____.

If you had lived when Jesus was a child, you probably wouldn't have played basketball, baseball, soccer, or even football.

But if you were a neighbor of the boy Jesus, you might have made up some other good games to play. The soil is dry where Jesus lived. There are little rocks on the ground. Can you think of a game you might have played?

Dear Jesus,

Sometimes it's hard to remember You grew up. Knowing You were once my age makes me feel _____ _____. I'm glad You grew up to be my Savior. Amen.

God showed His love for us.
1 John 4:9

A Bouncy Picture

Noah stood in front of the mirror. He was practicing different looks. Hold your hands up in front of you and pretend with Noah. Your hands can be a mirror.

You just jumped into a cold pool. You look _____ _____.

Your balloon popped. You look _____ _____.

You just stepped off the merry-go-round. You look ____ _____.

You're starting to get the sniffles. You look _____ _____.

Maybe you can play that game later using a real mirror like Noah. A mirror is just glass with special paint on the back. Light bounces back and forth, back and forth, from the mirror to you. That's how you can see your picture.

When you look in a mirror, you will see someone whom Jesus loves. Go to a mirror now. Find out whom Jesus loves.

Dear Jesus,
Thank You for loving me. Amen.

The Feel of Colors

This wasn't much fun. Brennan decided she really did not like the art museum. It was just walking from one room to another looking at things. Some of the paintings didn't even look like pictures!

Aunt Marie said ooh at this one. Then she stood for a long time looking at another before she smiled a big smile.

"What are you looking at?" Brennan asked. "All I see is a bunch of yellow and orange paint."

"People use colors to tell feelings," Aunt Marie said. "How do you think the artist felt who painted that?"

"Happy," said Brennan. "Orange and yellow are happy colors."

"What color would you use to paint how you feel now?" Aunt Marie asked.

"Blue and purple because I don't like this place," said Brennan. "Those are boring colors when they're mixed together."

If you painted a picture of Jesus, what colors would you choose? Why?

Dear Jesus,
Pink is a _____ color.
Blue is a _____ color.
Green is a _____ color.
When I think of You, I think of _____
_____ because _____.
Thank You for this colorful world. Amen.

May my words and my thoughts
be acceptable to You.
Psalm 19:14

All Kinds of Weather

Answer these questions about the weather.

Today is a great day to go to the beach. The weather
is _____.

This is a great day to get a suntan. The weather is ____
_____.

This is a good day to use an umbrella. The weather
is _____.

Today is a good day to play baseball. The weather is __
_____.

This is a good day to talk to Jesus. The weather is ____
_____.

There are some things you can only do in certain kinds
of weather. One thing that is nice about praying is you can
always talk to Jesus. If the sun is shining, if the wind is
blowing, even if the rain is falling, He will listen. Jesus
will always hear your prayers.

Dear Jesus,
 Today's weather was _____
____. Tomorrow the weather might be _____
_____. It's always a good day to pray.
Amen.

We will sing and praise Your power.
Psalm 21:13

Handy Hands

Instructions: Act out the devotion with your child.

My hands can do so many things.
They fly so high to be my wings.
My fingers reach to tap my toes
And then go up to touch my nose.
My hands together, they can pound
And then together touch the ground.
My hands swing here and then that way,
But most of all, my hands can pray.

Dear Jesus
   I usually pray when _____
____. When I fold my hands, I feel _____
_____. Thanks for listening to what I say. Amen.

Hear me, Lord, and be merciful.
Psalm 30:10

A Problem Day

Look up at the sky. How would you describe the weather today?

At Troy's house the sky was very blue this morning. Then it turned cloudy. Now it's raining. Troy can't go swimming.

Troy was going to play with Philippe. But Philippe isn't home.

Troy is hungry now. So his brother got out the peanut butter jar, a knife, and some bread. Troy tried to make a sandwich.

"I can't do it because of the lumps," Troy complained. "The peanuts make lumps in the peanut butter."

Poor Troy. He started to cry. "It's a problem day," he cried. "All I have is problems."

Have you ever felt like that? What do you do when you have problems?

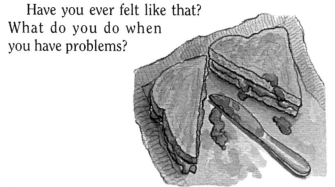

Dear Jesus,

I know You will listen when I tell You about a problem. One problem is _____.
Amen.

He rules over the sea, which He made.
Psalm 95:5

Bumpy Water

Kendra raced down to the lake. Watching the water was one of the best parts of vacation. "Look, Grandpa," Kendra said. "God made bumpy water today!"

"Well," said Grandpa. "I'm not sure God made the lake all bumpy."

"Zoom, zoom" went the roar of a motor. Then there were lots of waves. What do you think made those waves?

Kendra felt a cool breeze. Do you think the wind caused bumpy water?

"Oh, look," said Kendra. "Did you see that big fish jump? That made a big splash."

"Come on, Grandpa," said Kendra. "I want to go swimming so I can make bumpy water too."

Use your hands to show how Kendra splashed in the water.

Dear Jesus,

    Thank You for water. Water is fun to _____ _____. On a hot day, water is good for _____ _____. Today, I used water to _____. Thank You for water. Amen.

All of them depend on You to give them food.
Psalm 104:27

Eat Up a Circle!

"What's for lunch, Dad?" asked Ricardo.

"I'm hungry," said Norberto.

"Well, that's good because we're having a great lunch," said Dad. "Now boys, go and get the beach towels and lay them on the floor in a circle. We're having a round picnic inside today."

Their dad spread out the pizza dough. Make a circle with your arms to show how big the pizza might be.

Then Norberto added round pieces of sausage. Make a circle with your fingers to show the size of the sausage pieces.

Ricardo helped his dad flop a round gelatin mold on a plate. Make a circle the size of a gelatin mold.

"Hey, Dad, this is fun," said Norberto. "I thought it was going to be just another boring meal."

For dessert, the family ate something that's round and grows on top of the ground. It has seeds in it that you don't eat. What did they have for dessert?

What would you eat for a round meal at your house?

Dear Jesus,

Thanks for surprises. One of the best surprises I ever had was _____. One thing isn't a surprise, though: You love me. Thanks, Jesus. Amen.

He sets the time for sorrow and the time for joy.
Ecclesiastes 3:4

God's Time, My Time

Benjamin felt very sad. He felt very alone. Benjamin had just come home from his grandmother's funeral.

"Mommy, tell me again, why did Grandma die?" he asked.

"Her heart just stopped," Mother said. "God probably just said, 'Benjamin's grandmother, it's time for you to come to heaven.'"

"But it wasn't my time for her to die," said Benjamin.

Benjamin started to cry again. He missed his grandmother so much. His heart felt so empty.

Do you know anyone who died? Talk about it with the person sharing this book.

Dear Jesus,

Sometimes things don't happen when I want them to happen. You must have a calendar that's different from mine. Please help me remember that You are in charge and You really do know what is best for me. Amen.

He lives in union with God.
1 John 4:15

I Can Hear You

Whisper the words: "Jesus loves me."

Now say these words loudly: "Jesus loves you." Yelling those words would be one way to tell people about Jesus. But that might not be the best way.

Ears are special. You can't see inside your ears, but God made our ears with a long tunnel that leads to a drum. It's not a drum you'd hear in a band. It's called an eardrum. There are teeny, tiny bones inside our ears too. Loud noises can hurt those little ear parts.

That means yelling, "Jesus loves you," isn't a very good idea. Do you think whispering, "Jesus loves you," is a good way to tell people about our Savior?

Try whispering the words, "Jesus loves you." How many people heard you?

What are some ways you can tell more people about Jesus?

Dear Jesus,

I have a good idea of how to tell people about You. Now I need to think of who doesn't know You are the Savior. I will tell these people about You: _____
_____. Amen.

My Lord and my God!
John 20:28

Pairs

Let's play a game of things that go together.

A cup goes with a _____.

A pencil goes with _____.

A beach towel goes with _____.

A baseball cap goes with _____.

There are many right answers to these riddles. Things can be put together in different ways. Here are some other riddles.

Heaven goes with _____.

Love goes with _____.

Jesus goes with _____.

You probably had more right answers. It's fun to play with words, especially when you know there are lots of right answers. Even when we talk about Jesus, there are many ways you could answer that riddle. See how many different ways you can finish: Jesus goes with _____

_____.

Dear Jesus,
    Jesus goes with you. Jesus goes with me.
    Jesus goes with Grandpa. He goes with all three.

    That's 'cause He is Lord, Our Savior and our King.
    He gives us His love So that we can sing:

    Jesus loves you. Jesus loves me.
    Jesus loves everyone That you can see. Amen.

That should be enough for us.
1 Timothy 6:8

A Boring Vacation?

Darren looked out the car window. More fields! This was the most boring car trip ever, he thought. Yesterday all he saw was fields of corn. Corn, corn, and more corn. Today his dad said the fields were planted with wheat. Wheat, wheat, and more wheat.

"This is boring," said Darren. "No mountains, no lakes, nothing pretty to look at." What do you do in the car when you're bored?

"Well, Darren, these fields might not look real interesting, but you can be glad farmers have worked hard to plant all that grain," said Dad. "We need wheat and corn."

Think what you ate today and yesterday. How many times did you enjoy foods made from those grains? Darren thought of the meals he had eaten. Then he realized corn and wheat are important.

"You know, Darren, Jesus might have even eaten foods made from these same plants," said Dad. "When we stop tonight, let's see if we can look in the Bible and find out about that."

You can learn what people ate in Bible times too. Just look in Genesis 41:46–49.

Dear Jesus,

Thank You for giving me all kinds of different foods. My favorite thing to eat that's made with corn is _____ _____. My favorite wheat food is ____ _____. Amen.

Be kind and tender-hearted to one another.
Ephesians 4:32

What Can I Give?

Lori Ann had a problem. She wanted to give her grandfather a birthday present. But she didn't want to use all the money in her piggy bank. Have you ever felt that way? What do you think Lori Ann could do?

Lori Ann finally decided on something she could give her grandfather. She didn't go shopping at a hardware store. She didn't shop at a grocery store. She didn't shop at a clothes store. She didn't spend any money at all. But Lori Ann felt very good about her gift. What do you think she gave her grandfather?

Dear Jesus,

Sometimes I think I have to buy things to make people happy. Help me remember I can give a gift of love by ＿＿＿ ＿＿＿＿＿＿＿＿＿＿＿＿＿＿＿＿＿＿＿. I can give a gift of happiness by ＿＿＿＿＿＿＿＿＿＿＿＿＿＿＿＿＿＿. I can give a gift of time by ＿＿＿＿＿＿＿＿＿＿＿＿＿＿＿＿＿.
Thank You for Your gift of heaven. Amen.

God, be merciful to us and bless us.
Psalm 67:1

It's Summer

In summer the weather is hot.

In summer the weather is sweltering.

In summer the weather is _____.

What's another word for summer weather?

Sometimes several words can mean almost the same thing. What are some words you can think of for Jesus?

Dear Jesus,
    I can call You Savior
    Of earth and heav'n above.
    You are friend and God to me,
    My Lord so full of love. Amen.

I am there.
Matthew 18:20

Look Around

What a beautiful day for a picnic. Aaron leaned back against the tree trunk. He smiled at his dad.

"Where is God?" Aaron asked.

"God is everywhere," Dad answered. Aaron looked up. He saw big puffy clouds. What do you see when you look up?

Aaron looked left. He saw two girls playing catch. Now you look left. What do you see?

Aaron looked to the right. He saw a girl struggling to get her kite up in the sky. Now you look to the right. What do you see?

"Are you sure God is around here?" Aaron asked his dad again.

"He's promised to be with us," said Dad. "That's a wonderful feeling for me. I know I'm never alone."

Dear Jesus,
Sometimes I don't think of You being right here with me. Help me remember that when I feel lonely. Amen.

The Son of Man [Jesus] is Lord of the Sabbath.
Matthew 12:8

All on a Sunday Morning

Here's a story you can tell. Just fill in the empty spaces.

It was Sunday morning and time to get ready for _____ _____. The child first picked out some _____to put on. Next came the _____.

Now, all dressed, it was time for eating _____ _____.

Today it was a favorite meal, too: _____ _____. It tasted so _____.

Now it was time to leave for _____ _____. The temperature was so hot already this morning nobody needed to wear a _____ _____ or _____.

Everyone's ears perked up when they heard the ringing of the _____. That meant church was about to _____.

This is the story of one child's Sunday morning. In what ways is yours the same?

Dear Jesus,
     Sunday is _____.
Sometimes the week goes by so fast, I can hardly believe Sunday is here again. One thing I especially like about Sundays is _____. Amen.

183

Ever since you were a child,
you have known the Holy Scriptures.
2 Timothy 3:15

What's Ahead?

"What was I like when I was little?" Brandon asked his mom.

"Oh, you were cute," she answered. "I remember how tired I got picking up your toys. You had so much fun tossing them down. Then you laughed when I picked them up.

"Now I have a question," said Mom. "What do you think you'll be like 10 years from now?"

"Maybe I'll wear glasses like you," said Brandon.

"What do you think you'll be like 20 years from now?" Mom asked.

"Maybe I'll have a beard like Daddy," Brandon answered. "That would be funny."

"Well, I know one thing that will be the same," said Mom. "You will still end every day with Jesus. Years from now you might even say some of the same prayers we say now."

Talk to an adult about the prayers they said when they were younger. Do you know some of the same prayers?

Dear Jesus,

It's the end of another day. It's time to talk to You. Thank You Jesus for _____.
Help me, Jesus, to _____.
Amen.

A cloud cools a hot day.
Isaiah 25:5

It's Too Hot

August is often one of the hottest months of the year. What is the temperature outside at your house today?

Finish these sentences with hot-weather answers.

It's too hot to eat chocolate. If I tried to eat a candy bar, the chocolate would _____.

It's too hot to ride my bike. If I rode for just a little while, I would feel _____.

It's too hot to _____.

You can do lots of other things on a hot day. If you are inside where it might be cooler, take a small blanket or a couple of towels. Can you make a cool hideaway or even an igloo? take a cool drink and look at a book? What else can you do on a hot day?

Dear Jesus,

Sometimes summer is just no fun. It's too hot. I wonder what You did when You were little and the weather was hot. Maybe You wore sandals on Your feet. Did You make mud pies with dry earth and water from a well? I wonder if You _____
_____. Thanks for growing up, Jesus, to be my Savior. Amen.

A thousand years to You are like one day.
Psalm 90:4

Nothin' Special

"Now, Dana, you must be well-behaved when the relatives get here," said Mother. "Remember, this is a grown-up party."

"This is no fun," said Dana. "Won't Grandma even have candles on the cake?"

"Grandma's too old for candles," said Mother. "We'd have to buy boxes and boxes of candles."

"Won't Grandma get any presents?" Dana asked.

"Grandma doesn't want anything new," said Mother. "It's a treat for her just to have everybody together."

"Won't anything be like a real party?" Dana asked.

"Well," Mother thought. "We'll sing 'Happy Birthday,' and we'll thank God for another year. We do that for everybody's birthday."

"That doesn't seem special enough," Dana said sadly. "We can talk to God any old time."

Do you ever feel like that?

Dear Jesus,

Sometimes You seem so much like a best friend that talking to You doesn't seem special. But I know You are my Savior. That means You are the best friend of all. Amen.

Whoever loves Me will obey My teaching.
John 14:23

Skywriting

Consuela loved to swing. Back and forth, back and forth. She looked all around. Way up high she could see a tiny dot of an airplane. It was starting to write something.

"Miguel, Miguel," she called to her brother. "Come and look at the sky."

The two of them stood and watched the airplane. They tried to read what the letters said. But by the time the first word was finished, the letters were starting to disappear.

"Let's play skywriter," Consuela said. "You write something in the air, and I'll guess what you're writing."

Miguel took his finger and traced some letters in the air. You can play with him. Take your finger and write your name in the air. Now write the name of someone you like. Can you draw a heart shape too?

If you could really skywrite, you could put "Jesus loves you" in letters across the summer sky. But it will be a few years before you can do that. How can you tell people about Jesus right now?

Dear Jesus,
Help me be a good helper for You by _____.
Amen.

Let us bow down and worship Him.
Psalm 95:6

A Walking Lap

"Grandma, can I sit on your lap?" Jared asked.

"Wait until I finish the dishes," Grandma said. "You can be with me here."

"Grandma, can I sit on your lap now?" Jared asked.

"After I hammer this nail into the chair," said Grandma. "You can stand right next to me."

"Grandma, can I sit on your lap now?" Jared asked.

"I need to do a little touch-up painting," Grandma said. "You can come to the basement with me."

Jared started to cry. He sobbed, "Grandma, I don't want a walking lap. I want a sitting lap."

Have you ever felt like Jared that adults are too busy to spend time with you?

There are always things to do. Think for a moment: What are five things adults do where you live?

That's one thing that's nice about this book. Someone can sit down with you. You and someone else can spend time together with Jesus. And remember: When someone at your house has a lot to do, you can always talk to your friend, Jesus.

Dear Jesus,

People at my house get busy doing _____ _____. I am busy sometimes too. I like to _____. I'm glad I spend some time with You, Jesus. That makes me feel _____ _____. Amen.

All the nations see His glory.
Psalm 97:6

Sssssummer

Summer is full of things that start with the letter *S*. See if you can figure out some summer words.

What you wear for swimming: _____.

What you can find on a beach:_____.

What you do in a pool: _____.

What you wear to protect your eyes: _____.

What you wear to play in the yard: _____.

What you call quick summer rains: _____.

Summer is full of *S*. There's another word that starts with *S* that is important all year long. That word is Savior. Jesus is our Savior, yours and mine. That's important to remember all summer and autumn, winter and spring too.

Dear Jesus,

Thanks for shells and sand and sunglasses and other fun things of summer like _____ _____. Thank You for being my Savior now and all year. Amen.

Be kind.
Ephesians 4:32

What Can I Do?

Tell what you would do.

Daddy had his arms full of groceries. The screen door was closed. I _____.

My friend and I were swinging. She put her feet down to stop the swing, but she fell. I _____ _____.

A wave came far up on the beach. My friend's sand castle tumbled down in the water. I _____ _____.

The girl next door dropped a penny in the grass. She started to cry. I _____.

My friend doesn't go to church. The next time I see him, I _____.

Dear Jesus,

Help me be loving and kind to others. Remind me that helping people learn about You is a very important job, but it's something I can do well. Amen.

Continue to grow.
2 Peter 3:18

Growing Up, Growing Old

There sat Grandma. She had a small scissors in one hand. Sure enough, she was clipping her nails!

"Grandma, do your nails grow?" Latasha asked.

"Well, of course, I have to cut my nails," Grandma answered. "I may be old, but my nails still grow."

"Does your hair still grow?" Latasha asked.

"Of course," said Grandma. "I just got it trimmed again last week."

"How else do you grow?" Latasha asked.

"I grow fat if I eat too much of your daddy's barbecued chicken," laughed Grandma. "Just because I'm growing old doesn't mean I can't grow inside too."

"Inside?" Latasha asked. "I don't understand."

"I learn so much going on my trips," said Grandma. "And I will always keep growing with this."

Latasha's grandma picked up a Bible. Latasha knew her grandma read it every day.

"Come here, honey," Grandma said. "You can learn today too."

What can you learn from the Bible?

Dear Jesus,

I know a lot of things. I also have a lot to learn. Help me learn more about You as I grow up. Amen.

In every church service I want the [people] to pray.
1 Timothy 2:8

It's Easy

Is it easier for you:
To brush your hair or brush your teeth?
To hold a bat or hold a fork?
To float on your stomach or float on your back?
Each of us is different.
Can you wiggle your ears? Some people can.
Can you stand on your head? Some people can.
Can you pray easily to Jesus? Some people can.

Others have trouble talking to Jesus. Praying doesn't need to be hard. You just start by saying, "Dear Jesus." He will always listen to what you want to say.

And here's something else: The more you pray, the easier it is! That's nice to know.

Prayer suggestion: Talk to Jesus about your day.

God loved the world so much that
He gave His only Son.
John 3:16

Around the World

Instructions: Act out the devotion with your child.

Here's a little game for moving around. Show how you would get around on a hot desert. How would you move across a lake? Now pretend you are crossing some slippery ice—be careful!

We can move in many different ways. People hear about Jesus in all kinds of ways too.

Some people learn about Jesus when they hear a song. What song do you know about Jesus? Some people learn about Jesus when someone sits down and tells them. Have you ever told someone about Jesus?

Other people learn about Jesus when they read the Bible. Ask an adult to help you find John 3:16 in the Bible. Reading that verse is how some people learn about Jesus.

How did you first learn that Jesus was your Savior?

Dear Jesus,
    Thank You for letting me learn about You. Help me share Your Good News with others. Amen.

I pulled him out of the water,
and so I name him Moses.
Exodus 2:10

Camp-Time Games

Emily loved to go camping. She and her brothers played a game all the way to Rock Lake. One child would act out something about camping. Then the other children would guess what it was. You can play with Emily too.

Put your hands together, as if you were holding a pole. Now look down and see if you can see a bobber moving. What are you acting out?

Now pretend to pick up a piece of wood, now another and another. Can you carry your heavy load? Don't drop the wood on your foot!

Now Emily is sitting like she's holding a book. You can sit like that too. She's very quiet. What are you acting out?

Emily's family always takes the Bible on vacation. Each night, before it gets too dark to read, a child chooses a favorite Bible story.

Tonight Emily knows what she will pick: the story of a baby who floated in a basket. Do you know that story? You can find it in Exodus 2:1–10.

Dear Jesus,

Sometimes in summer we can do special things and go new places. Something special for me this summer is _____ _____. One place I visited was _____. Thank You for summer. Amen.

Even if the seas roar and rage.
Psalm 46:3

Yucky Water

Emily and her family had almost reached Rock Lake. What a great place to camp! The car stopped and Emily raced to the water. She always liked to watch the little fish. But this wasn't right! She couldn't see through the water.

"The water's too thick," Emily called to her older brothers. "I can't find fish."

The boys came to the shore. Corey read the big sign. "This water has been judged unsafe. Do not drink. No swimming. No fishing."

"Corey, what happened to my fish?" Emily asked. "Why did God put old water in the lake?"

"He didn't, Emily," Corey said sadly. "Everything God does is perfect. People polluted Rock Lake."

Emily started to cry. She and her brothers walked slowly back to the car.

"Oh, Daddy," Emily cried. "God needs to turn on the clean water faucet. The water is all yucky. There aren't any fish."

Emily was angry. Emily felt sad. She was disappointed. How do you feel after hearing this story? What would you say to Emily?

Dear Jesus,
    You have made a beautiful world. Please help me take good care of my corner of the earth. Amen.

Let us go to the Lord's house.
Psalm 132:7

Let's Go!

See if you know what these places are.

There's water here. People splash. Your feet sink into sand. People sit under umbrellas. This place is a _____ _____.

There are animals here from all over the world. You can see monkeys climb, laugh at seals barking, and buy a hot dog to eat. This place is a _____.

It's noisy here! Rides go around on the ground and around in the air. There are lots of people. Things cost money. This is a _____ _____.

It's quiet here some of the time. People sing here. People pray here. People see friends here. They go here on Sundays. This place is a _____.

There are many wonderful places to visit. Some places we don't visit often. Churches are good places to visit. We can go to church often. When do you go to church?

Dear Jesus,

I like to go to church because _____ _____. I know in church I will hear that You love me, forgive me, and are my Savior. Going to church helps me remember those important things. Amen.

Look down from heaven at us.
Psalm 80:14

Flying through Heaven?

Sasha was taking her first airplane trip. She was spending every minute looking out the window. Sasha watched all the suitcases roll up into the plane. Then she looked out as the plane taxied to the runway. Finally in the air, everything looked so small beneath them. But Sasha still looked out the window.

All she saw were bunches of big fluffy clouds. The clouds were like big marshmallow puffs. This isn't what heaven was supposed to look like, Sasha thought.

"When do we see heaven?" Sasha asked, tugging on her mother's sleeve.

"We don't know where heaven is," said Mother.

"But I thought heaven was in the sky," Sasha said. "Aren't we going to fly at least near heaven today?"

"Oh, Sasha, there's so much we don't know about heaven," said Mother. "The Bible says that heaven is a wonderful place where we will be with God. But I don't think we'll fly through heaven on this trip."

Sasha thought about that a moment. She really had wanted to peek into heaven. Well, that was okay, Sasha thought. When she got home, she would pretend to take her dolls on a trip to heaven. How do you picture heaven?

Dear Jesus,
Heaven seems so far off. That's why I like it that You are close enough to always listen to me pray. Amen.

How good it is to give thanks to You, O Lord.
Psalm 92:1

Away from Home

Julie and her family were sitting in a restaurant. Julie thought that eating at different places was one of the best things about vacation. While they were waiting for their food, Julie's dad asked what everyone had liked best about the day.

"I liked the museum with the big bones," said Kyle.

"I liked the place where we could push all the buttons," said Julie.

"And, Seth, what about you?" Dad asked.

Seth sat quietly. He was thinking. "We're seeing too many famous places," he finally said. "I want to go home."

"We'll be home in just a few more days," said Dad. "Then you can sleep in your own beds."

Seth brightened up when their food was served. His hot dog looked almost like the ones he ate at home.

"Now let's pray," reminded Dad. "We're away from home, but God travels with us."

Dear Jesus,

Thanks for staying with me even when I'm away from home like _____. Amen.

Go and work in the vineyard today.
Matthew 21:28

Whose Hat?

What kind of hat would each person wear?

An astronaut: _____.

A construction worker: _____.

A motorcycle rider: _____.

A welder: _____.

A deep-sea diver: _____.

A chef: _____.

A magician: _____.

Sometimes a hat gives a clue to a person's job. Now think for a minute. As a worker for Jesus, what kind of hat would you wear?

Take a long piece of paper and make a band that will fit around your head. Draw pictures of what you do as Jesus' helper.

Prayer suggestion: Talk to Jesus about your work for Him.

You belong to God.
1 John 4:4

Almost

Instructions: Every time you hear the word *almost*, start to give a person a hug—but don't finish it!

Drip, drip, drip. The rain was slowing up. It had *almost* stopped. Soon Sara could go outside and play.

"Come and work on your room while you're waiting for the rain to stop," called her mother. "You *almost* finished cleaning it yesterday."

The rain stopped. Sara finished cleaning her bedroom. Now it was time to play in the puddles. But one foot was stuck, just when she *almost* had her boots on.

Sometimes *almost* seems like a word that isn't finished. When Jesus says that He loves us, it's not an *almost* kind of love. Jesus loves us when we make mistakes. Jesus loves us when we do things wrong. His love isn't *almost*. His love is like a big hug—now finish your hug. That's what Jesus' love is like!

Dear Jesus,

You can't hold me in Your arms to show that You love me. But You are my Savior. That's how I know You love me. Amen.

See how much the Father has loved us!
1 John 3:1

Park and Park

Jesse was just learning to read. That's what made this vacation such fun. He could read some of the signs when the family drove through new towns.

"Park" he read happily.

"Park" he read again. "Where are the swings, Mommy? The sign says, 'Park.' "

"It's great you can read that word," laughed Mom. "But 'Park' on those signs means to stop the car. It's not a place for children to come and play."

Some words mean different things. But some words only mean one thing.

Mommy means love.
Sister means love.
Jesus means love.

We can use those words in different ways, but they always mean the same thing: Someone loves you.

Dear Jesus,

I know that You love me. Other people love me, too, like _____. You love me as my Savior. Amen.

God looked at everything He had made,
and He was very pleased.
Genesis 1:31

Creation Chains

"Grandma, are you going to read the Bible again?" Kari asked. "I thought you finished it yesterday."

"I read the Bible over and over," said Grandma. "Since Grandpa died, I've read the whole Bible more than 40 times."

"Is that so you won't get bored like us?" Kari asked.

"Are you two bored again?" asked Grandma. "I'll tell you what. You can listen to me read a while and then make a chain using the colors from the story I read."

Kari and her brother listened as Grandma read the story of creation. But Kari didn't hear anything about colors. All she heard about was God making water and trees and birds.

"Now you think about what I read," Grandma said. "I'll go and get some colored paper for strips."

"But, Grandma, that wasn't a colorful Bible story," complained Kari.

"Just think of all the things you heard that God created," said Grandma. "Then pick out two or three colors of things and make a 'creation chain' to decorate the living room."

Kari picked blue for the sky and green for the grass. Her brother picked red for cardinals, green for dandelions, and brown for tree bark. They worked all afternoon on their creation chains. Can you make one too?

Dear Jesus,

Thank You for so many wonderful things in the world especially _____. Amen.

Praise the Lord's glorious name.
Psalm 29:2

Summer Sounds

Splash, splash. Water lapped at the sides of the boat.
Where do you think Jenny is?

"Hooray! A home run. Hooray!" Where could Lisa be?

"Jesus loves me, this I know." Where is Ola?

"Come home by 5 p.m." Where could Ana be going?

"Stay out of the seaweed." Where is Lauren?

Sounds of summer are all around. Listen carefully. What summer sounds do you hear?

Dear Jesus,

   Summer sounds are warm and comfortable. At this time of year, I especially like _____.
Amen.

Come with Me, and I will teach you to catch men.
Mark 1:17

Hunting for Friends

Here is a thinking game. Which of your friends:

Can ride a bike: _____.

Has a pet dog: _____.

Likes bubble baths:_____.

Has a summer birthday: _____.

Eats pancakes: _____.

It's fun to know so many people. It's neat to think how everyone is different.

Many of your friends might be the same in some ways too. Think of the people you just mentioned. Do they all live in the same town? ride in cars? shop at stores? know about Jesus?

That's very important. If someone doesn't know about Jesus, how can they find out? Can you help?

Dear Jesus,
   Some people are different.
   Some people are the same.
   Help me now, dear Jesus,
   To tell my friends Your name. Amen.

God is the one who ... created the winds.
Amos 4:13

Feel the Wind?

Instructions: Move with your child like the wind when the word is said.

Ross loved visiting the farm at this time of year. It was almost time to harvest so the cornstalks were very tall and dry. The *wind* whistled through the rows of stalks.

"Uncle Eddie," Ross asked. "Don't you just love the *wind?*"

"It sure feels good today," Uncle Eddie said. "That *wind* keeps me cooler out here in the hot sun."

"God made the *wind* to do lots of things," said Ross. "It blows my pinwheel."

"When the old *wind*mill was working, a good stiff breeze made those arms turn just like your pinwheel," said his uncle.

Ross looked up at the bright blue sky. Big, puffy white clouds slowly crossed the sky. What was making them move? Act out your answer.

Dear Jesus,
Thank You for wind. Wind moves a sailboat across ____ _____. Wind blows leaves from the _____ that I can run in. Wind lifts a kite high in the _____ _____. When I feel the wind, I remember that You are in control of our world. Thanks, Jesus. Amen.

*Every good gift and every perfect present
comes from heaven.*
James 1:17

A Dog Day

Erin and her puppy, Max, came inside the house and plopped down. Erin was sweating. It was a hot day to run. Her dog lay down with its mouth wide open, breathing fast. It was a hot day for a dog to run too.

"Why, Erin, you're dripping wet," said Grandma. "Why were you running on such a hot day?"

"Max and I were chasing each other," said Erin.

"I can tell," said Grandma. "Poor Max will take a while to cool off."

"He's just breathing a lot," said Erin.

"That's how a dog gets air-conditioned," said Grandma. "It's called panting."

Can you pant like a dog? Erin tried. She opened her mouth and took lots of fast breaths. Try it. Are you cooler?

"Grandma, it doesn't work for me," said Erin.

"Of course not," Grandma said. "You cool off by sweating. Dogs cool off by panting. They take lots of fast breaths to get out all the hot air. Then the cool air can come in."

"Wow," said Erin. "Did Max think of that?"

"No," said Grandma. "God planned it all."

Dear Jesus,
Thank You for helping me keep cooler by _____ _____. Amen.

We are going to worship the Lord.
Zechariah 8:21

Packing Up to Go

Let's pretend you're going swimming. What are two things you'll need?

Let's pretend you're going to watch a baseball game. What will you take along?

Let's pretend you're planning a picnic. What will you take?

Packing up—and unpacking—are things we do a lot during the summer. That's because summer is a good time to do things and go places.

There's one place you don't have to pack anything to visit. You don't need a backpack or a suitcase or even extra socks. It's just important you come to this place. Of course, you can always bring a buddy. Do you know what place we're talking about?

Dear Jesus,

I know You're glad to see me come to church. I know You'll be glad to see any friends that I bring too. Amen.

Thank You, Jesus

Instructions: Act out the devotion with your child.

Sometimes praying can be quiet time alone with Jesus. Sometimes people pray and talk out loud. This is an action prayer.

Pretend to catch a basketball, jump a rope.

Thank You, Jesus.

Pretend to throw a pass, roller-skate.

Thank You, Jesus.

Pretend to kick a football, sing a song,

Thank You, Jesus.

Pretend to juggle three balls, ride a bike.

Thank You, Jesus.

Dear Jesus,

I'm glad I'm growing up and can do so many neat things. Thank You, Jesus, for helping me grow. Amen.

I am like a wild bird.
Psalm 102:6

Whoo! Whoo!

Chikako loved this special time of the evening. Her grandpa would walk with her around the park looking for birds and animals.

Sometimes they saw creatures that squiggled. How would you squiggle?

Sometimes they saw creatures that flapped. How do you flap?

Sometimes they saw animals that paraded on a leash. How would you walk attached to a leash?

Tonight it was very quiet. Chikako held her grandpa's hand. Then, she heard, "Whoo, whoo." Can you make that sound?

The sound came from up above them. What do you think it was? "Whoo, whoo." Chikako was very scared and hugged her grandpa tightly.

"Oh, Chikako, that's our first owl," Grandpa said. "We've never heard one here before."

"Grandpa, why did God make owls? That scared me," she said.

"I'm very glad God made owls," Grandpa said. "Owls help catch those pesky mice. God knew just what He was doing."

Dear Jesus,

I like lots of animals. I especially like animals that crawl like _____, that run fast like _____, and birds that _____. Thanks, God, for all the different kinds of creatures in the world. Amen.

His love is eternal.
Psalm 118:1

A Family Tree

"Mommy, I want to do something," Rachel said. "It's so boring without the kids."

Rachel's big sisters had gone off to school. Rachel's school hadn't started yet. She had nothing to do and nobody to play with. "I miss the girls," Rachel said.

"Make them something," Mother suggested. "Draw a picture of our family."

"I can't draw feet," Rachel complained. "My feet are always funny looking."

"Then make a family tree," said Mother. "Then you only draw the faces. I'll help you."

Her mother drew a tree with one branch for each member of the family. Then she drew a circle at the end of each branch.

"Now, Rachel," Mother said, "you fill in the faces."

Rachel worked hard. She colored everyone's eyes just the right color and put a bow in the hair of one of her sister's just like she always wore. She even drew glasses on her mother. But when she was done with her family faces, there was still one circle left. Who was missing? Then Rachel knew. Rachel talked softly, almost to herself.

"Sorry, Jesus," Rachel said. "I was feeling so sorry for myself today I almost forgot about You."

Can you make a family tree too?

Dear Jesus,
    Thank You for my family: _____
_____. Amen.

I call you friends.
John 15:15

Lunch-Box Friend

Michael picked up the lunch box from the kitchen table. He walked slowly to the front door. He liked school. But today, the first day of school, he wasn't so sure he wanted to go.

"Have a great day," said Grandmother. "And when you open up your box at lunch, you'll find a surprise."

The morning went quickly. Michael liked his new teacher. It was great to see his old friends. But Michael still felt a little lonely.

At noon he pulled out his lunch box. Inside, on the lid, was a picture of Jesus. Michael smiled.

Just then John came by. John said, "Hey, wanna be friends?"

"Sure," said Michael. "I've got a friend already, but I always like more."

What friend was Michael talking about? Do you know anyone who might like a lunchtime friend tomorrow?

Dear Jesus,

Thanks for being my friend. Thanks for some other neat friends like _____. Amen.

We find protection under the shadow of Your wings.
Psalm 36:7

I'm Thinking

Here's a word game to play using the names of people in the Bible. You may have played this before using other things or people. Let's start.

I'm thinking of a baby in a basket. His name was ____ _____.

I'm thinking of a man who built a zoo that floated. His name was _____.

I'm thinking of a lady who had a baby on the first Christmas. Her name was _____.

I'm thinking of a boy who had a slingshot. His name was _____.

Now you make up a line.

I'm thinking of _____.

Dear Jesus,

Today I'm thinking of people in the Bible. I'm thinking about _____. I often think about You. Amen.

Seek your happiness in the Lord.
Psalm 37:4

Just Right

Here's a pretending game. You are going to help make things "just right."

First pretend to take a large spoon to stir some pudding. Be careful not to touch the hot pan! That's just right!

Now help mix some nuts into cookie dough. The dough is stiff. You'll have to work hard. There, just right!

Help to cool a glass of orange juice. Drop in some ice cubes, one at a time. Be careful so the juice doesn't splash out of the glass. One, two, three ice cubes. That's just right!

Now think about a person who is just right. This person loves Jesus. This is someone who tries to learn more about Jesus. This is someone who talks to Jesus in prayer. This person tells friends about Jesus. Who is this?

You! You are just right for Jesus.

Dear Jesus,

I know I'm not perfect and I make mistakes, but thanks for Your love. I'm glad I'm just right for You. Amen.

Men and animals are in Your care.
Psalm 36:6

Which Chick?

Christopher liked to visit the children's zoo. That's where he could see farm animals. The chickens were his favorites. Today he stood at the fence and looked at a hen and her chicks.

"Does the mother name her baby chicks?" Christopher asked.

"No," said Dad.

"How does she know which chick is which?" Christopher asked.

"I don't really know," said Dad. "She says cluck, and they come, I guess."

"I'm glad you know my name," Christopher said.

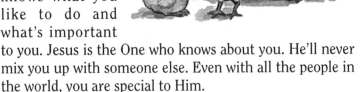

There's someone else who knows your name. He knows all about you too. He knows what you like to do and what's important to you. Jesus is the One who knows about you. He'll never mix you up with someone else. Even with all the people in the world, you are special to Him.

Dear Jesus,

I'm glad I am so special to You. You are special to me too. Amen.

Go and preach.
Matthew 10:7

 abc

Who Helps Jesus?

Amy Marie was quiet as her family drove home from church. She didn't understand what the pastor had said.

"Mommy, Pastor Rogers said everybody should work for Jesus," Amy Marie said. "Why isn't everybody a pastor?"

"There are lots of different jobs," said Mother. "Even though I work at the hospital, I try to be one of Jesus' helpers."

"And I do that at school too," said Dad. "Pastors work all the time for Jesus."

"So you're just a part-time helper?" Amy Marie asked. Her parents laughed.

"I guess you could say that, honey," said Dad. "We try to act like Jesus would want us to wherever we are."

Who are people who work all the time for Jesus that you know? Who works part-time for Jesus?

Dear Jesus,
    I try to be a good worker for You by _____
_____. Amen.

How I love Your law!
Psalm 119:97

All Kinds of Books

There are many kinds of books. Even if you're just learning to read, you probably know all about books. See if you can answer these questions.

If you want to find out where someone lives, you can look in a _____.

If you want to find a recipe for chocolate chip cookies, you can look in a _____.

If you want to sing a song, you look in a _____
_____.

If you want to find out about Jesus, you read the ____
_____.

The Bible is a special book. The Bible is God's book. It has stories about people who really lived. In the Bible, you can learn about people who loved God a long time ago.

You will learn how to read all kinds of books. But the most important book you will learn to read is the Bible.

Dear Jesus,
To me, the Bible _____.
I can learn about You from the Bible. Amen.

Sing a new song to the Lord.
Psalm 98:1

Finger Counting

First count all your fingers. Now sing the song "Ten Little Indians."

We're going to use your fingers and the tune you just sang. Here are some new words that you can sing to "Ten Little Indians." Count on your fingers as you sing.

One little, two little, three little children;
Four little, five little, six little children;
Seven little, eight little, nine little children;
Ten who all love Jesus.

Now use your fingers to help you count 10 children whom you know. Sing the song again. As you sing and count, think of those friends who love Jesus.

Dear Jesus,
    Thank You for my friends like _____
_____. Thank You for being a best friend too.
Amen.

Before the world was created,
the Word already existed.
John 1:1

An Adopted Grandpa

"Daddy, how old is Grandpa Hank?" asked Matthew.

"He's 59," said Dad.

"How old is Dee Dee?" Matthew asked.

"Your grandma is 59 too," said Dad.

"That's not old enough," Matthew said. "My teacher said the kid with the oldest grandparent would get a special prize. Mine aren't old enough."

"Well, Matthew, there's not much you can do about that," said Dad. "Where are you off to now?"

"I have to draw pictures of any grandparents I have," said Matthew. "Then I have to write their ages under the pictures."

Matthew worked with his crayons for a long time. Then he drew a big 59 under his grandpa's picture. Matthew put a big 59 under his grandma's picture. Under another picture he wrote 1,000,000,000,000, ... until the zeros ran off the page!

Matthew's dad came and looked over his shoulder as he put away the crayons.

"Very nice," said his father. "Grandpa Hank and Dee Dee would like their pictures. But who is this one?"

"I adopted Jesus for a grandpa," Matthew said. "I only have two grandparents, and some kids have more. So I figured I would adopt Jesus. Nobody's older than He is."

What do you think of Matthew's idea? Can you draw pictures of your grandparents?

Dear Jesus,

Thank You for giving me people who love me like ____
_____. Amen.

*We ourselves know and believe the love
which God has for us.*
1 John 4:16

Nice Words

Think of the nicest thing anyone ever said to you. What was it? How did you feel about hearing that?

Jesus has nice things to say to each of us. He tells us: I will always love you. I forgive you when you make a mistake. I am your Savior.

Can you say something nice to someone right now?

Dear Jesus,
    When I hear that You love me, I _____
_____. I'm glad You forgive me when I
_____. Amen.

*Whoever believes that Jesus
is the Messiah is a child of God.*
1 John 5:1

A Jesus Train

Cory went right to his room after Sunday school. He needed to finish his picture. The teacher had told the class to "draw people whom Jesus loves." Cory only had time to finish three people.

"Mommy, can I have another piece of paper?" Cory asked.

"Sure," she said. "Help yourself."

"Mommy, can I have some tape?" Cory asked.

"Sure," she said. "Help yourself."

Cory drew more people.

"Mommy, can I have another piece of paper?" Cory asked.

"Sure," she said. "You know where it is."

"Mommy, can I have another piece of tape?" Cory asked.

"Cory, what in the world are you doing?" Mother asked.

"Mr. Morrison said to draw pictures of people Jesus loves," Cory explained. "I need more paper to draw more people. I tape the papers together. See my Jesus train?"

Cory had already taped together pieces of paper that made a long strip. Can you make a Jesus train too?

Dear Jesus,
I am glad You love me. Amen.

I am telling you the truth.
John 5:24

Measure It

Alika found a worm wiggling on the sidewalk. How can she measure how long the worm is?

Tim went to the doctor for a checkup. How could the doctor tell how much he weighed?

Derek watched his dad in the kitchen. He needed two teaspoons of cinnamon for the recipe. How would he get the right amount?

Rulers, scales, and measuring spoons are fun to use. After you are done with this page, you can measure how tall you are or weigh yourself.

But some things can't be measured. One thing we can't weigh on a scale is Jesus' love. His love is longer than all the rulers in your house.

Think for a moment about Jesus' love for you. Then talk to Him about His love.

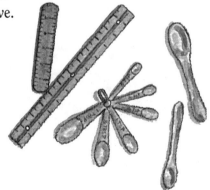

Prayer suggestion: Tell Jesus how You feel about His love.

I will trust in You.
Psalm 55:23

I Can Do It!

Clap your hands three times every time you hear something you can do.

Throw a ball.
Jump up and down.
Share a toy.
Eat politely.
Hop on one foot.
Help at home.

You can do many things. There's something else you can do: thank Jesus. He has helped you grow up this far. He will be with you as you keep growing. You can count on that. You can count on Jesus.

Dear Jesus

I'm growing up. Sometimes it's _____
_____ being _____
years old. I can't wait till I'm _____
_____. Then maybe I can _____
_____. Thanks for sticking with me. Amen.

I look at the sky, which You have made.
Psalm 8:3

A Pretty Bedtime

"Mommy, Mommy," Benito called. "See the fluffy sunset? Come and look out my window."

"Benny, it's way past your bedtime," called Mother. "No more stalling. Get back to bed."

"No, no," Benito said. "You have to come see. God really must have worked hard on this."

His mother walked into the room. The sky was lovely. Fluffy pink clouds floated against the blue.

"I told you God did a good job tonight," said Benito. "How did He paint that?"

"Oh, Benny, it's not painted," said Mother. "The colors are just reflected, like in a mirror."

"Isn't it pretty?" Benito asked.

"Yes, honey," smiled Mother, "but it's also time for bed."

Look out your window tonight before you climb into bed. What colors do you think you'll see in the sky?

Dear Jesus,

Thank You for the colorful world. My favorite sky colors are _____. When the sky looks gray, I think the weather will be _____ _____. When the sky is clear blue, I think the weather will be _____.
Amen.

You have given me [joy].
Psalm 4:7

Clap, Clap, Clap

Clap one time for each of the seasons. Did you clap four times? We have spring, summer, fall, and winter.

We're going to play a clapping game. Clap once if you see this thing just in one season. Clap twice if you have this thing in two seasons, and so on. Ready to clap?

Snowsuits
Colored leaves
Easter baskets
Christmas trees
Baseball games
Ice-cream cones

Some things are around all the time. Others we have only for a short time during the year.

We celebrate Jesus' birthday just once each year. But He is with us every single day. We celebrate Easter just one Sunday each year. But the meaning of Easter—that Jesus is our Savior—is important all the time.

Dear Jesus,

Some things, like my birthday on _____ _____, are special because they come just once a year. You're special, Jesus, even though You are with me all the time. Amen.

I am worn out, O Lord.
Psalm 6:2

Troubles

"I'm starving," Sean told his father.

"It's still an hour until supper," Dad replied. "Maybe you better have a muffin."

"I want a Popsicle," Sean said.

"It's a muffin or nothing," said Dad.

Sean took a muffin. This had been a rotten day, he thought.

"Be sure you take the muffin out of the paper before you take another bite," said Dad. What do you think had happened?

Sean peeled off the rest of the muffin cup.

"Now my muffin is all broken up," he cried. "And look at the blueberries inside. I hate blueberries."

Sean sat at the kitchen table and cried.

Have you ever felt like Sean? What do you do when things don't go well?

Dear Jesus,

Things don't always work my way. Help me remember patience when things don't go right. I hope I remember You are nearby to listen to my problems. Amen.

You have been good to me.
Psalm 13:6

Mark the Place

Has this ever happened at your house?

It was time to read *Little Visits Every Day*. Bryan looked for the right page. He remembered some of the pictures, but he couldn't find the last devotion he had heard.

"What's the right page, Mom?" Bryan called. "I can't find it."

His mom came over to Bryan. She paged through the book too.

"Tell you what," she said. "Let's make a bookmark just for *Little Visits Every Day*. Then we'll always know where to turn."

You can do that too. Cut a piece of paper into a strip. Use a ruler to measure if you'd like.

A piece of paper about 2" wide and 6" long works well.

What will you draw on your bookmark?

Dear Jesus,
    I look forward to my time with You. I especially like
_____. Amen.

When You give them breath, they are created.
Psalm 104:30

Me

Instructions: Act out the devotion with your child.

Let's pretend that I'm a tree
God planted in the ground.
My feet can be the roots to dig
Down deep where water's found.

My body is the strong, tall trunk
That's standing up so straight.
I take my hands to feel the bark,
A skin that God did make.

Watch my arms move to and fro
As branches they are now.
They start to move a little more
As strong winds start to blow.

I can pretend, and it is fun,
To be a strong, tall tree.
But I am really God's own child;
I'm me, I'm me, I'm me.

Dear Jesus,
I know I am special. I do things with my arms like
_____. I use my legs
to _____. I am your
special child. Amen.

Under the apple tree ....
Song of Songs 8:5

Kissed by God

It was apple pickin' time where Jenny lived. Now she could ride a wagon through the orchard. Today was when she'd drop apples—*plunk*—into her big bag. It was apple pickin' time! Today Aunt Dorothy was coming along. Apple pickin' would be more fun than ever.

"How do you know when it's ready to pick?" Aunt Dorothy asked Jenny.

"When an apple turns ripe-ish you pick it," said Jenny.

"How does ripe-ish look?" Aunt Dorothy asked.

"Oh, a little bit reddish," said Jenny. "It looks like God kissed it." *Plunk, plunk.* Ripe-ish apples dropped into the bottom of the bag. Now Jenny carefully laid the apples on the next row. The bags were heavy in no time at all. Apple pickin' didn't last long.

Aunt Dorothy turned to Jenny. "Your face looks a little ripe-ish too, Jenny," Aunt Dorothy said.

Jenny felt where the sun had warmed her cheeks. It was a nice feeling to think she had been kissed by God. Have you ever felt that way too?

Dear Jesus,

Help me remember these warm autumn days next winter when I'm cold. Even when the weather turns cold, help me remember I can always be warmed by Your love. Amen.

The Lord will take delight in you.
Zephaniah 3:17

Happy Birthday!

Birthday cards can say many different things.

A funny birthday card might make you laugh. It might read _____.

A birthday card can tell you someone likes you. This kind of birthday card might say _____ _____.

A birthday card can look very fancy. A fancy card might have on it all kinds of _____.

You can make a birthday card using _____ _____.

Jesus never sends birthday cards. But He gives us good things and good people and good food all year. Jesus is glad you were born. Do you think He smiles in heaven on your birthday?

Dear Jesus,
    My favorite thing about birthdays is _____ _____. Amen.

Teach a child how he should live.
Proverbs 22:6

Lots of Questions

Megan was going to have her tonsils taken out. She asked many questions. "Mommy, are they going to put my tonsils back in?" Megan asked.

"No, honey," said Mother.

"When they take out my tonsils, how will I breathe?" Megan wondered.

"Tonsils don't help you breathe," said Mother. "You don't need tonsils to breathe."

"Tonsils remind me of ambulances," said Megan.

"You won't ride in an ambulance," said Mother. "I'll drive you to Dr. Grabau in our car."

Megan's mother was glad she was asking questions. The answers would help Megan learn.

Some children like to know about life when their grandparents were young. Other children want to learn how airplanes fly. Adults can help you find answers.

If you have questions about Jesus, adults can help you too. Who else could help you learn more about Jesus?

Dear Jesus,

Thank You for giving me people who teach me about You like _____. Amen.

How wonderful it is.
Psalm 133:1

So Big

"How big was I as a baby?" Ian asked his dad.

"Oh, about so big," Dad said. He held his arms apart just a little bit. Ask an adult to show how big you were as a baby.

"How big was I when I was two years old?" Ian asked.

"Oh, about so big," Dad said. He held out his arms a little wider. Ask an adult to show how big you were as a two-year-old.

"How big was I when I was three years old?" Ian asked.

"Oh, about so big," Dad said. He held out his arms a little wider. Ask an adult to show how big you were as a three-year-old.

"How big was I …?" Ian started to ask.

"You're big enough now for a nice hug," Dad said. He stretched out his arms even wider and gave Ian a big hug. Can you do that, too, with someone now?

Jesus' love for you is big too. Stand with your arms stretched way out. That's how big Jesus' love is for you.

Dear Jesus,
Thank You for loving me so much. Amen.

Let us sing for joy to God, who protects us.
Psalm 95:1

Thanks, Anytime

The rain fell steadily. It wasn't raining hard. It wasn't raining softly. Just raining. It was a gloomy day.

Laurie watched her mother read the newspaper. Her mother glanced up. She smiled. "Let's say thank you to God," Mother said.

"It's not lunchtime yet," said Laurie. "It's not bedtime."

"But I feel like thanking God now," said Mother.

"For what, rain?" Laurie asked.

"No," said Mother.

"For an umbrella?" asked Laurie.

"No," said Mother.

"For what then?" Laurie asked.

"That we're here together, safe from the weather, just the two of us," said Mother. "I'm grateful to God."

Think for a moment. For what are you thankful right now?

Dear Jesus,
    Thank You for _____.
Amen.

God has the last word.
Proverbs 16:1

Good-bye and Hello

Sergei carried his swimsuit to his mother. He sighed.

"It's a good-bye time," he said sadly. "No more swimming till next year."

His mother looked up. She put her arm around his shoulders. "Remember every time there is a good-bye, a hello is at the other end," she said. "Why just look at those bare feet. They are wiggling hello to your new school shoes."

Sergei looked down. He wiggled his toes. Can you make your toes wiggle hello to autumn?

"And when the wind blows away the colored leaves of fall, you can say hello to snowflakes," Sergei's mother said.

"And next spring I can say good-bye to my mittens and hello to stomping in spring puddles," Sergei said, smiling.

"That's right," said Mother. "God has planned every good-bye with a hello."

What things from the summer do you put away now? What fall things are you saying hello to?

Dear Jesus,

I guess that's my hello to You. Talking to You like this helps me feel _____. And when I say Amen, that's good-bye. Amen until tomorrow.

God will put His angels in charge of you.
Psalm 91:11

Peekaboo Pal

Instructions: Act out the devotion with your child.

Hold your hands in front of your face to play peekaboo. Now try it once—open your hands: peekaboo. Every time you hear those words in this story, play peekaboo. This is the game Kari was playing with her friend Angel. Let's listen.

"Peekaboo," said Kari.

"Peekaboo," she said again.

"Whom are you playing with?" Dad asked.

"My friend Angel," said Kari. "We're playing peekaboo,"

"But I don't see anyone," said Dad.

"Daddy, I have a secret," Kari whispered. "Angel is real only to me."

"Oh?" asked Dad.

"Everybody else has a brother or sister," Kari said. "You told me Jesus sends an angel, so I play with Angel. She likes peekaboo."

"Well, I like that game too," said Dad. "Peekaboo!"

Dear Jesus,

Thank You for watching over me. Thank You for sending angels to help take care of me. Amen.

All of them depend on You.
Psalm 104:27

Tails

A dog curls up with tail around
When it is time to sleep.
A fish's tail goes back and forth
To help it swim so deep.

The oppossum hangs from toe to head
So high up in the tree.
The little ducks swim tail to tail
For that's all that they can see.

A piggy's tail is quite a sight
All curled up in a knot.
The peacock's tail spreads like a fan
With color all about.

A monkey's tail is there to help
It swing from tree to tree.
God made some animals with tails,
But there's no tail for me.

God created you and me
To tell about His Son.
The Lord Christ Jesus, loves you so,
I say to everyone.

Dear Jesus,
    Help me tell my friends about You. Amen.

How happy are those who live in Your Temple.
Psalm 84:4

Houses

Look out the window. Do you see a red house? a house with a brown roof? a building that is tan?

What shape are the windows you can see: round? square? rectangular? What shape is the window you're looking out of right now?

Houses come in all sizes and shapes and colors. So do churches, God's houses. Think about your church. Is it big? Are the windows plain or fancy?

Now think about what you do in church. That's what is really important. Can you pray to God? sing songs about Him?

Dear Jesus,
    When I go to church, I like _____
_____. My church is special because _____
_____. Amen.

You alone, O Lord, keep me perfectly safe.
Psalm 4:8

Time for Bed

It was time for bed. But Justin wasn't in bed. He walked to his mother's room.

"Justin," said Mother. "Go back to bed."

"Your bed is warm and cozy," said Justin.

"Justin, go back," Mother repeated.

"I feel sleepier in your room," Justin said.

"Justin," said Mother. "Go to your bed now."

"I'm lonely," said Justin.

Have you ever felt like Justin? Here's a prayer you might use next time you feel alone at bedtime.

Dear Jesus,
When it is dark, I worry
Of things that frighten me.
May I remember You're right here,
With me You'll always be. Amen.

Walking for Jesus

Instructions: Stand up with your child. Every time you hear the word *walk*, take a step forward.

If I had been a little child
When Jesus was on earth,
I could have *walked* to Bethlehem
To hear about His birth.
I could have *walked, walked, walked* to Jesus.

If I had lived as long ago
As Jesus when He preached,
I could have *walked* the countryside
To hear our Savior teach.
I could have *walked, walked, walked* to Jesus.

If I had been there when He told
Of God in heav'n above,
I could have *walked* to all my friends
And told them of His love.
I could have *walked, walked, walked* for Jesus.

I wasn't there when Jesus lived
Those many years ago.
I couldn't *walk* to tell my friends
About His love, but now
I'm glad to *walk, walk, walk* for Jesus.

Dear Jesus,
Help me be a good helper for You. Amen.

Praise the Lord.
Psalm 134:1

Thanks, Jesus

Instructions: Help your child fill in the blanks.

On an umbrella day, the weather is _____ _____. On an umbrella day, I would like to _____. I can thank Jesus for an umbrella day.

On a windy day, it is fun to _____ _____. On a windy day, I would like to _____ _____. I can thank Jesus for a windy day.

On a bright day, the sun usually _____ _____. On a bright day, I would like to _____ _____. I can thank Jesus for a bright day.

Today is a _____ day. I would like to _____.
I can thank Jesus for this kind of day too.

Prayer suggestion: Talk to Jesus about something you would like to do or did already today.

He does whatever He wishes.
Psalm 135:6

Time to Collect

"Come on, Sara," said Grandfather. "We need to collect more firewood."

"Look at that squirrel collecting nuts," said Sara.

"That's what autumn is all about," said Grandfather. "Time to collect."

"Is Barney collecting bones to dig up in winter?" Sara asked.

"I doubt it," Grandfather laughed. "But he might be growing a few more hairs in his coat to protect him from the winter cold."

Grandfather and Sara worked hard. Then it was time for a rest.

"Yup," said Grandfather. "Autumn's a time for collecting. My favorite thing to collect in fall is thoughts."

"Thoughts?" asked Sara.

"Sure," said Grandfather. "All spring and summer and fall I save up memories. Then when it's a cold winter day, I just enjoy my thought collection."

Sara wasn't sure what her grandfather meant. But she tried to collect her thoughts of the other seasons. Collect with Sara: a special feeling about spring; a wonderful thing that happened this summer; some fun you've had this fall.

Dear Jesus,

Help me remember in winter the good times of spring when _____, of summer when _____, and talking to You on this autumn day. Thank You, Jesus. Amen.

Feed yourself spiritually on the words of faith.
1 Timothy 4:6

Inside the Cover

"Mommy, where's your Bible?" LaRona asked.

"Go look on the dresser in the bedroom," Mother said. LaRona found it. Mommy's Bible had a white cover with a zipper.

"Why is your Bible different from Grandma's?" LaRona asked.

"It's the same," said Mother.

"But Grandma's is black and has gold on the pages," said LaRona. "Yours is white with a zipper around it."

"Oh, that's just the cover," said Mother. "What's inside is the same."

"When can I have a Bible?" LaRona asked.

"Well, I guess when you learn how to read," Mother answered. "Yes, that's when. And we can have your name put on the front."

"Oh, thanks," said LaRona. "I want one with a pink cover."

"We'll see about that," said Mother.

How many Bibles do you have at your house? Do they all look the same on the outside? How would you use a Bible?

Dear Jesus,

I think about the Bible as a book for older people. But soon I'll be old enough to read one too! That will be ____ _____. Amen.

See how much the Father has loved us.
1 John 3:1

I'm Special

Instructions: Help your child fill in the blanks.

I'm special.
I like to _____.
My hair is _____.
And Jesus loves me.

I'm special.
I'm good at _____.
I laugh when _____.
And Jesus loves me.

I'm special.
My friend is _____.
We like to _____.
And Jesus loves us.

Dear Jesus,
I know I am special to You. That makes me feel _____
_____. Amen.

Praise Him, … all animals.
Psalm 148:9–10

Finny, Feathery, Furry

Here's a pretending game.

Jump like one of the animals God created. What animal were you pretending to be?

Fly like one of the birds God created. What creature were you playing?

Swim like one of the creatures God created. What were you swimming like?

Move on four paws like one of God's four-legged animals. What animal were you pretending to be?

God created many wonderful animals in this world. Some have fins, others, feathers or fur. Think for a moment about your favorite animal. Then talk to Jesus.

Dear Jesus,

My favorite animal is _____
because _____. I also like
things that swim like _____
and fly like _____.
Thanks, Jesus, for furry, feathery, and finny things. Amen.

God is the one who has
prepared us for this change.
2 Corinthians 5:5

Bury a Treasure

Instructions: Act out the devotion with your child.

Scamper, scamper. The squirrel raced around the yard. Now she paused. The nut in her mouth was getting uncomfortable. Where could she hide it?

Scamper, scamper. She tried to dig her front paws into the ground by the swing set. No. She scraped the brown grass back in place. The squirrel looked around.

Scamper, scamper. Now to the back gate. That won't work. Scamper, scamper. By the sand pile!

The squirrel dug furiously with her two front paws. Drop. Into the hole went the nut. Now the squirrel covered up the buried treasure.

Animals everywhere are getting ready for winter. How are you preparing for a new season?

Dear Jesus,

Animals seem to know just what to do for winter. Thank You for giving me people who will help me get ready for a new time of year. Amen.

I praise You, O Lord.
Psalm 119:12

J Words

Here are some riddles. All the answers are words that begin with the letter *J*.

Something that tastes good with peanut butter: _____ _____.

A word that means "leap up": _____.

A pumpkin with a face: _____.

The name of our Savior: _____.

Jesus is more than a word. Jesus was born to be our Savior. That's worth jumping up and down for! Try it.

Dear Jesus,

You really are wonderful. Thank You for being You. Amen.

I have provided ... [for all the wild animals].
Genesis 1:30

A Clothesbasket Turtle

Muneeza crawled underneath the clothesbasket. There! That made a cozy house. Now she crawled slowly down the hall. This was the life of a turtle, she thought. She crept up near her daddy.

"Hi, Daddy," Muneeza whispered from under the overturned basket. "I'm a turtle."

"Muneeza, you scared me!" said Daddy. "What are you doing under the clothesbasket?"

"I'm a turtle," she said. "I'm carrying my house on my back. Turtles don't need to clean out their drawers and put on winter clothes. I like being a turtle."

"Well, you might like being a turtle now," said Daddy, "but if we don't get the summer clothes out of your drawers, you'll be a cold little turtle when winter comes."

"I wish I were a turtle," sang Muneeza, and she crawled off down the hall.

How does God take care of turtles? Ask an adult to help you find the answer.

Dear Jesus,

You have such good plans for taking care of Your world. Thank You for giving me people who help me get warm clothes for winter. When I see how animals get ready for cold weather, I know for sure You are helping them too. Amen.

Come and see what God has done.
Psalm 66:5

What Color Is Autumn?

Sabrina loved autumn. She loved all the colors. She especially liked the bright colors on the Halloween decorations. Sabrina liked the orange colors she saw. What do you see that is orange in autumn?

Sabrina liked the brown she saw. What do you see that is brown in autumn?

Sabrina walked through the leaves on the ground. She liked the green colors she saw. What do you see that is green in autumn?

Sabrina shuffled through the acorns on the ground. She liked the golden colors she saw. What do you see that is golden in autumn?

Sabrina looked up. Her mother was standing at the front door waving a big red cloth. Sabrina is deaf; she can't hear. Her mother calls her by waving a red towel.

Sabrina ran eagerly toward the bright red color. That meant it was suppertime. She was hungry. What do you like that is red?

Dear Jesus,

Thank You for the colors of autumn. My favorite fall color is _____ because _____

_____. Amen.

The Lord alone—is our God.
Deuteronomy 6:4

One, Two, Three...

There are numbers all around us. Can you see any from where you are sitting? Now think a moment. Where would you find numbers in the kitchen? in the garage? in the bedroom?

There are even numbers in the Bible. Ask an adult to help you find the answer to these questions.

How many helpers did Jesus have? (*Mark 3:14*)

In how many days did God create the world? (*Genesis 1:31*)

How much food did Jesus have to feed the people? (*Mark 6:41*)

Numbers tell us "how many." How many years old are you? A number will be your answer.

Dear Jesus,

There is only a single number I need when I think about You: number one. You are the one and only God. Amen.

Our God is compassionate.
Psalm 116:5

Tough Times

I can't do this; I won't do that.
I might as well not try.
I couldn't win; I know I can't.
I think I'll sit and cry.

Some things are hard; they just won't work,
And then it isn't fun.
I'll grump around without a smile
Until the day is done.

When shoes won't tie, my bike falls down,
And it's a lousy day,
Help me remember "can't" and "won't"
Are not good words to say.

As Jesus' child, I make mistakes.
I might not always win.
But He has promised, with His love,
To take away my sin.

Dear Jesus
    Thank You. Smiling isn't always easy, but I know You love me. Amen.

The sun knows the time to set.
Psalm 104:19

Clock Talk

Look at a clock. Let's see what you can learn. Will it tell you the day of the week? Does your clock say it's October? What does your clock tell you?

Different clocks tell different things. Some are very fancy. Others don't have many numbers at all. When do you look at a clock?

Long ago people used the sun as a clock. You might even see a sundial sometime at a museum. Our modern clocks work well even on cloudy, rainy days!

What time do you usually get up? What time will you go to bed today? What time will you talk to Jesus? Setting a certain time to do things can be a good idea. What is your very favorite time of the day?

Dear Jesus,
      My time for You is _____.
On Sunday, my time for You is _____
_____. That's a good time because _____
_____. Amen.

Remember your Creator while you are still young.
Ecclesiastes 12:1

Squeaky Hinges

"What are you doing?" Fernando asked his grandmother.

"With all the rain we've been having this fall, some of these door hinges get a bit squeaky," she said. "I'm just trying to get out the squeaks."

Grandmother pulled the door back and forth. *Squeak, squeak.*

"It's a good thing your hinges don't make noise like that," laughed Grandmother.

"What hinges?" asked Fernando.

"Bend your knees," said Grandmother. She listened. "No. No squeak there. Your hinges are really called joints."

Bend your knees with Fernando. Do your joints squeak? Then Fernando listened to some other hinges: his elbows. Do your elbows squeak?

How many squeaky doors can you find in your house?

Dear Jesus,

I really never thought about my knees and elbows. But they really work well. I can bend my knees if I kneel to pray. My elbows bend when I fold my hands. Thanks, Jesus, for all my hinges. Amen.

Darkness and light are the same to You.
Psalm 139:12

Two Eyes in the Night

Paolo was almost asleep. Suddenly he saw two eyes looking at him in the dark.

"Daddy, Daddy," he cried. "There's a Halloween ghost. Daddy, Daddy."

Paolo's father came racing into the bedroom and flicked on the light. There was Whiskers, the cat, sitting on the bed.

"Oh, Paolo, that was just Whiskers," Dad said.

"But Whiskers' eyes were so bright," said Paolo.

"That's because God made cats with special eyes. Light bounces off them to work like a mirror," explained Dad. "That helps cats hunt for food when it's dark.

"Come, now, get to sleep," said Dad. "Think of Jesus. His eyes are full of love for you. Now close your eyes, and good night."

Do you ever worry about things in the night? What helps you go to sleep?

Dear Jesus,

When I am afraid at night, help me remember that You take care of me. Sometimes I get scared of _____ _____. Help me remember that You are with me. Amen.

The Lord protects me from all danger.
Psalm 27:1

No Mask for Me!

Instructions: When you and your child hear the word *mask*, put your hands over your eyes to make masks.

"I'm not wearing a *mask* for Halloween," Heather told her mom. "It's too scary behind a *mask*."

"Well, that's fine, honey," Mom said. "Actually this is one time when it's probably better if you don't wear a *mask*."

"You mean it's good to wear a *mask*?" Heather asked.

"Sure," Mom said. "Some people need to wear a *mask* when they go to work."

Heather thought for a minute. "Dr. Johnson," Heather said. "She sometimes has a *mask* around her neck at the hospital."

She thought some more. "And that man that fixed our furnace for winter," Heather said. "He wore a big *mask* when he used that fire."

"Yes, a welder wears a *mask*," Mother said. "Even astronauts wear a sort of *mask*."

"I'm still not wearing a *mask*," Heather said. "I'm just going to pretend to wear one. I'll put my hands over my face and say boo. Then people will still know it's me."

Do masks ever scare you around Halloween? Talk about that to the person reading this book. Then talk to Jesus.

Dear Jesus,
Sometimes masks help people at their jobs. Sometimes masks are silly. Sometimes masks scare me, especially
_____. Please help me remember You are always with me. Amen.

They rejoice in what You have done.
Isaiah 9:3

That Neat Orange Ball

Instructions: Act out the devotion with your child.

Pretend to do this with Deka. Hold a big orange ball—be careful! Don't drop it. This is heavy. Now set it on a table.

Now hold it steady while an adult cuts a hole in the top. Look inside. Do you see all the seeds? Now you're ready to scoop them out. What were you acting out? Have you cleaned out a real pumpkin at your house?

What can you do with a pumpkin? Some people roast pumpkin seeds and eat them. Do you do that? Some people like pumpkin pie. Is that one of your favorites? Some families like pumpkin soup. That is delicious. So is pumpkin bread. Look in a recipe book. Find some foods to make with pumpkin.

Deka's family eats pumpkin pudding. But that's not her favorite thing about pumpkins. She likes to make pumpkins into jack-o'-lanterns. What do you like best about pumpkins?

Dear Jesus,

You make many wonderful things. One of the best is a pumpkin. I like the pumpkin's skin, which feels _____ _____. Pumpkin seeds taste _____ _____. But the best thing about pumpkins is _____.
Thanks, Jesus, for pumpkins. Amen.

When I am afraid, ... I put my trust in You.
Psalm 56:3

Scary Halloween?

It's almost Halloween at Patrick's house. How do you feel around Halloween?

"Halloween sure is great," said Patrick's dad.

"Well, I guess," Patrick said slowly. "But I really think Halloween is scary."

"Scary?" Dad asked. "You kids just put on costumes and masks."

"But sometimes I think the masks look real, and then I get scared," Patrick said. "Halloween isn't fun at all."

"What else scares you?" Dad asked.

"I dream about the scary costumes," said Patrick. "I keep thinking about them."

"Is that all?" Dad asked.

"That's enough," said Patrick. "Halloween is just awful for me."

How can Patrick's dad help him? What do you do when you are afraid? Whom can you talk to about your fears?

Prayer suggestion: Talk to Jesus about things that frighten you.

I love you just as the Father loves Me.
John 15:9

Jack-o'-lanterns

Martin walked by all the jack-o'-lanterns. Some looked really good. Would his happy-face pumpkin win the contest?

"Gather around, everyone," the announcer said. "It's time to award the jack-o'-lantern contest ribbons."

"For a spooky-face pumpkin, the winner is Jake," the announcer read. "Jake's card says this is a ghost." Can you make a spooky face?

"Winner for the best jack-o'-lantern with a surprised expression is Kendra," the announcer said. "Kendra's card says this is how she looks when she opens a present." Can you look surprised?

"Winner for the best happy-face jack-o'-lantern is Martin," the announcer read. "Martin's card says this is how he feels because he's loved."

Martin walked up to the stage for his ribbon. He smiled a big smile. He knew he was loved. His mom loved him. His sister loved him. Jesus loved him. Martin smiled as big as his pumpkin smiled.

Think of those who love you. Does your smile show you are loved? Let's see your smile.

Dear Jesus,
Thank You for loving me, all the time, every day. I love You too. Amen.

What a rich harvest Your goodness provides!
Psalm 65:11

It's Autumn

Carlos looked up. He could tell it was fall. What do you think he saw?

Carlos listened as he shuffled along. He could tell it was fall. What do you think he heard?

Carlos sniffed. He could tell it was autumn. What do you think he smelled?

Carlos reached down to pick up a sign of autumn. What do you think Carlos held in his hand?

The weather is changing. Fall is here. Look out your window. What signs of autumn do you see?

Dear Jesus,

I can tell fall is here. It's a new month, November. There are changes outside like _____

_____. I even dress differently than I did in summer. Now I wear _____. I know You'll listen to me in every month of the year. Amen.

Let your praise be heard.
Psalm 66:8

Open Up for Jesus!

Instructions: Act out the devotion with your child.

Let's pretend to open up things. Use your hands. Ready?

Open a present.

Open a closet door.

Open a garbage can.

Open a bag of potato chips.

Now just open up your mouth! That's how easy it is to tell people about Jesus. You don't need a can opener, garage door opener, or even a letter opener. You just can open your mouth and tell somebody about Jesus.

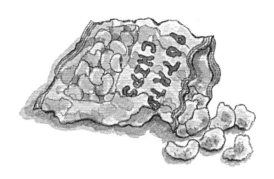

Dear Jesus,

Sometimes I'm afraid to tell people about You. I think that maybe _____. Help me remember that You'll help me tell others about You. Thanks for the help. Amen.

A child lies quietly in its mother's arms.
Psalm 131:2

Who's Special?

"Mommy, I need cuddle time," Matthew said. He climbed onto his mother's lap. They just sat quietly. The weather outside was gray and cloudy.

"When I grow up, I won't sit on your lap," Matthew said.

"That's true," said Mother.

"When I grow up, I'll be so busy we won't have cuddle time," Matthew said.

"You're probably right," said Mother.

"But I'll still love you," said Matthew.

"Of course," said Mother.

Who is a special person in your life? Draw a picture for this person. Then ask someone to help you write today's date. Your special friend might want to save the picture and remember the day you drew it.

Dear Jesus,

You are special to me. Other special people are _____
_____. I love these special people and You. Amen.

Every ruler on earth governs with My help.
Proverbs 8:16

A Vote for Jesus

Alphonso was going to vote. He wasn't going to do the voting, just walk along with his grandpa. They went together to a little room. It was barely big enough for both of them. Alphonso couldn't see what was going on. His grandpa was studying something. He frowned. He smiled. He closed the little book. Grandpa was finished.

"Well, that's what voting is," Grandpa said as they started walking home. "You pick the people who will do the best job."

"I guess you voted for Jesus, then," Alphonso said. "He's the only one who's perfect."

"You're right about that," Grandpa said with a smile. "We try and try and still aren't perfect. We just do the best job we can."

"Will the people you picked do a good job?" Alphonso asked.

"I hope so," Grandpa said. "I always pray for people at election time. I don't pray that my friends will win. I just ask God to help our leaders do a good job."

Dear Jesus,
I try to follow the rules. Sometimes I don't do as well as I could. Thank You for always forgiving me. Please be with people who are in elections like _____
_____. Help them do a good job. Amen.

*Praise with one voice the God and Father
of our Lord Jesus Christ.*
Romans 15:6

Word Partners

Here's a word game with many right answers. See how many things you can think of that go along with each word.

Socks and _____.

Fork and _____.

Bat and _____.

Circus and _____.

Jesus and _____.

There are many words to pair up with Jesus. Did you say Jesus and me? Jesus and you? Jesus and church? Jesus and everyone? All kinds of answers would be right. That's one thing that's wonderful about Jesus: He's for everyone.

Dear Jesus,
I'm glad You are paired up with me. Amen.

I thank my God for you every time I think of you.
Philippians 1:3

Body Talk

Get ready to move! Your body is going to do some talking, but you won't even say a word. Ready?

Tell your elbows to relax. Now gently close your eyes. No peeking! Tell your fingers to walk down and touch your toes. Now wiggle those toes, but no talking.

Breathe deeply in and out. In and out. In and out. Don't say anything. Now open your eyes. Without saying anything, tell someone you like him.

Words can be wonderful, but sometimes you don't need to talk to say things.

Dear Jesus,
My body works so very well;
It does so very much.
I thank You, Lord, for hands and feet,
For parts of me that touch.

I feel the softness, hardness, bumps
Of all that You have giv'n.
I thank You, Lord, that one day, too,
I'll feel the joy of heav'n. Amen.

Ask and you will receive.
John 16:24

Time for the Dentist

"I don't want to see the dentist," Aaron said. "Luke and Phillip say it hurts."

"It never hurt me," said Aaron's big brother, Ryan. "Dr. Azar just counts your teeth. Then somebody else uses a toothbrush with a motor to make sure they're clean."

"Why did those guys say it hurts, then?" Aaron asked.

"Sometimes kids just try to scare little boys" said Ryan. "Besides, we need to take care of our teeth so we can chew."

"I don't know about that," said Aaron. "I could just drink milkshakes and eat ice cream. If God didn't give me teeth, I wouldn't need to go to the dentist."

"But then you wouldn't be able to talk very well either," said Ryan. "And you couldn't eat crunchy apples. And the tooth fairy wouldn't come."

Aaron thought about that last idea. He still hadn't lost a tooth, but there was one that wiggled.

"Come on, Aaron," said Ryan. "God knew what He was doing. He even gave us a dentist close by our house. Let's go."

Have big kids ever teased you? scared you? Remember, Jesus is a grown-up friend who will always listen to what you say.

Prayer suggestion: Talk to Jesus about what other kids say to you.

Forgive us our sins.
Luke 11:4

I'm Sorry

What makes these sounds? See if you can tell.

Buzz: _____.

Click: _____.

Rip: _____.

Chirp: _____.

Slam: _____.

Some of the hardest sounds to say are "I'm sorry." It's not easy to admit when we make a mistake. But we all make mistakes.

It's not easy to ask someone to forgive us. But it happens to each of us at some time. "I'm sorry" sometimes sticks on our tongues. "I'm sorry" is just hard to say.

Talk about those words with a grown-up. When is it hard for you to say, "I'm sorry"?

Dear Jesus,
When I tell You I'm sorry I did something wrong, I know You forgive me. Amen.

Your greatness is seen in all the world!
Psalm 8:1

God Knows Best

This would be a great trip to the zoo, thought Ashlie. It wouldn't be as crowded as in the summer. Maybe she could even get close to her favorite animals, the snakes.

Later that afternoon, Ashlie stood right in front of a snake. It was coiled in a circle.

"Mommy, do snakes hatch out of tummies?" Ashlie asked.

"No," Mother answered. "Snakes lay eggs."

"Do snakes make nests then?" Ashlie asked.

"Different snakes do different things," Mother said. "We can get a library book about that if you're interested."

"Well, if birds come from eggs and snakes come from eggs, why did I get born from you?" Ashlie asked.

"Because God planned it that way," Mother said. "God knows best."

"I guess that's right," Ashlie said. "You would have looked funny on a nest."

Talk to someone about your birth. Were you born in a hospital? Who came to visit you? What did you like to do as a baby?

Dear Jesus,
When I think of everything You planned and made, I think _____. Amen.

May He be pleased with my song.
Psalm 104:34

Let's Sing!

We are going to have some singing fun. First sing "Twinkle, Twinkle, Little Star."

That helped you remember the tune to the song. The new words we're going to sing fit perfectly with the melody of "Twinkle, Twinkle, Little Star."

I love Jesus; yes, I do.
He's a Savior for me and you.
When I do things that aren't right,
He forgives me day and night.
I love Jesus, yes, I do.
He's a Savior for me and you.

Jesus came from heav'n above
Just to share His great big love.
He can bring to everyone
Joy and peace till life is done.
Jesus came from heav'n above
Just to share His great big love.

Dear Jesus,
Thank You. Amen.

Let us go off by ourselves.
Mark 6:31

A Tired Day

Anne looked out the window. The sky was gray. A light rain was falling. She walked around her house. There was nothing to do, but that was all right. Anne didn't feel like doing anything. It was a tired day outside. Anne felt like it was a tired day inside too. She plunked down in a chair.

Everybody has tired days. Show how your hands feel when they are tired. Now make your arms feel tired. Now your shoulders. Relax your feet. Now let your legs hang limply. Do you feel tired too?

It's okay to feel tired. It's okay to relax your body. It's good for us to feel quiet sometimes. When Jesus was on earth, He rested too. What do you do that's relaxing?

Dear Jesus,

Thank You for times I can be noisy and busy like when _____. Thank You for quiet times, too, like when _____. I get tired when _____. Thank You for the gift of sleep. Amen.

It was the season when grapes were beginning to ripen.
Numbers 13:20

Fun Little Fruits

What is a kind of fruit? A fruit that is little? A fruit that is fun? Did you guess a raisin?

Keisha likes to eat raisins out of a little box. Barry likes raisin bread toast. If you lived in Bible times, you might have eaten a raisin cake.

Raisins are some of God's fun fruits. What are some other foods that are fun to eat?

Dear Jesus,

Some food is good for me like _____ _____. Some food is crunchy like _____ _____. Some food is just plain fun like _____. Thank You for food. Amen.

May the Lord be happy with what He has made!
Psalm 104:31

Here Comes Winter!

Winter's coming! I can tell because _____
_____.

Winter's coming! Winter is fun because _____
_____.

Winter's coming! In winter the birds _____
_____.

Winter's coming! The weather gets _____
_____.

Winter's coming! That means Jesus' birthday is _____
_____.

Dear Jesus,
    Thank You for an exciting new time of year. I especially
like _____. Amen.

You made summer and winter.
Psalm 74:17

The Last Leaf

One leaf. That's all that was left on the tree. One leaf left on the big tree. Pretend to be that leaf as a grown-up reads you this story.

The leaf fluttered. The wind stopped blowing. The leaf hung limply. A child whizzed by on a bike. The leaf moved slightly.

A few big drops of rain fell. The leaf flickered this way and that.

The wind started blowing harder. A storm was coming. The leaf twisted and twirled—now off the branch. The leaf floated down, fluttering, fluttering, all the way to the ground. It lay gently on the ground.

The leaf would lie there all winter. It would be part of a warm blanket for God's earth.

Dear Jesus,

Sometimes it seems just amazing how fall always comes after summer. How winter comes after fall. Every year it's like that. You are in charge all year round. That's how I know that after fall and winter, spring will come again. But now it's time for the earth to sleep. Amen.

Forgive the sins and errors of my youth.
Psalm 25:7

No Job Too Little

It was clean-up day at Joshua's house. Grandma was coming for a visit. Everybody needed to help. But Joshua didn't want to work. After all, he just had a little job. He was supposed to empty out all the wastebaskets. Nobody noticed when he slipped outside to swing in the cool, autumn air.

What a lovely day God had made! This was better than emptying wastebaskets, thought Joshua. He went swinging even higher. He could almost see, yes, there was Grandma's car pulling up.

Excitement filled the air. There were hugs and kisses, and even, yes, even presents. When everything had been opened, Joshua's brothers started to collect the wrapping papers and ribbons. They tried to stuff the scraps into the wastebaskets, but that didn't work.

What do you think happened next? You finish the story.

Dear Jesus,
Because I'm not very old yet, sometimes my work does not seem very important. But I know it's important that I do whatever job I'm given. One job I'm responsible for is _____. Amen.

God's people ... live together in harmony.
Psalm 133:1

Place Cards for Thanksgiving

Alexis was busy making place cards to use at the Thanksgiving dinner table. She had folded little papers in half. Now she was drawing a picture for the person who would sit at each place.

On the first paper, she drew a picture of someone driving a car. Whom would that be for in your family?

On the next one, Alexis drew someone cooking at the stove. Whom would that be for in your family?

Now she drew someone outside gathering sticks to use in the fireplace. Whom would that be for in your family?

Alexis worked for a long time. She was almost finished. The last place card she drew had a picture of a Christmas scene and a manger. Do you know whom that place was saved for?

At Alexis' Thanksgiving, one chair is always set for Jesus. This reminds everyone at the table who has given all the blessings. What do you think of that custom?

Dear Jesus,
Help me remember to thank You for _____
_____ and for _____
_____ and for _____.
But most of all, I thank You for being my Savior. Amen.

Everything shouts and sings for joy.
Psalm 65:13

The Meaning of Thanksgiving

"Willy, you can't play here," Erin complained. "You mess up everything."

"Get away, Wil," said Seth. "You're too little."

"Don't do that, Wil," Megan said. "You'll just get in trouble."

Wil sat and thought. Then he tromped into where his mom was working. "They aren't Thanksgiving me," he complained.

Wil's mom looked up. She put down the hammer. Fixing the chair would have to wait. "Children," she called. "Let's all go into the living room."

Seth, Megan, Erin, and Wil all sat down.

"It's time to teach Wil about Thanksgiving," Mother said. "Not about turkeys and relatives coming but about what Thanksgiving means."

The older children sat quietly. No one said anything.

"Wil gave a wonderful clue just now," said Mother. "He said you weren't 'Thanksgiving' him. What does the holiday really mean?"

See if you can find the meaning of giving thanks. Look at Psalm 65 in the Bible.

Prayer suggestion: Talk to Jesus about Thanksgiving.

Happy are those whom You choose.
Psalm 65:4

Nervous Shoes

Instructions: You and your child can make a squeaky sound when the word *squeak* is read.

Squeak, squeak. Sabrina wasn't sure she should have come. She had never been to a church.

Squeak, squeak. Her shoes were so new they made noise.

Squeak, squeak. What should I do in church? Sabrina wondered. Her friend had invited her to come. Jaime had promised to meet her here. But where was she?

Squeak, squeak. She tiptoed to the water fountain.

"Hello," said a smiling woman. *Squeak, squeak* went Sabrina's shoes as she backed away from the fountain.

"My name is Miss Miesner," said the woman. "What's yours?"

Squeak, squeak went Sabrina's shoes as she moved toward Miss Miesner to whisper her name.

"I'm Sabrina," she said quietly. "The squeak is just my shoes. They squeak when they're nervous."

"Don't worry," said Miss Miesner, smiling. "After you've worn them to church a few times they won't be squeaky nervous at all."

Let's pretend Sabrina is coming to your church for the first time. How would you make her feel welcome?

Dear Jesus,

Help me remember what it's like to be in a new place. When somebody new is at church, I can _____
_____. Amen.

We feast on the abundant food You provide.
Psalm 36:8

Eating Up the Centerpiece

Asha was having a grand time arranging fruit for the Thanksgiving centerpiece.

First she put some round red fruit into the horn of plenty. What did Asha choose?

Then she picked up some round orange-colored fruit. What did Asha use?

Now Asha separated some long, yellow fruit for the centerpiece. What kind of fruit was that?

Asha stood back and clapped her hands. The horn of plenty looked full.

Asha loved this part of Thanksgiving. When people came to the table on the holiday, everyone chose a piece of fruit. Then each person wrote on a little piece of paper one way in which God had blessed him or her during the year. The paper was stuck onto the fruit and put back in the cornucopia. At dessert time, Grandpa would read each blessing, then hand the fruit to the person who had written the thank You to God.

If you went to Asha's house for Thanksgiving, which fruit would you choose? What would you be thankful for?

Dear Jesus,
This Thanksgiving, I am especially grateful for _____
_____. Amen.

> Be fair to the needy and the helpless.
> Psalm 82:3

Thanksgiving?

Alex's nose was busy sniffing. The smell of turkey filled the house. Alex could still catch a whiff of the pies that had been baked this morning. He peeked into the kitchen. Mom and Grandpa were busy making his favorite salad.

But Alex wasn't happy. Tomorrow he would eat all these wonderful foods. But today his family was making a Thanksgiving meal for people who might be hungry.

"It's not fair," Alex burst into the kitchen. "I want Thanksgiving today."

His grandfather looked up. Then he went to the sink to wash his hands.

"Come here, Alex," Grandpa said kindly. "Now tell me, what day is tomorrow?"

"Thanksgiving," said Alex.

"You're right," Grandpa said. "But today can be Thanksgiving too. Today we can be glad we have so much food that we can share with others."

"You mean it's one of those Christian things to do, like you always say?" Alex asked.

"Yes," nodded Grandpa. "But the real Christian feeling has to be in our heart. Your mom and I are so grateful for so many things. We just want to share God's blessings with somebody else."

How do you feel about this story?

Dear Jesus,
Sometimes I really don't want to share. It's just hard to give. Help me remember what You give me. Amen.

He provides food for those who have reverence for Him.
Psalm 111:5

A Food Rainbow

"Now, Jenny, how did you like my Thanksgiving salad?" Grandma asked.

"Oh, I didn't have any," said Jenny.

"Our pet turtles eat more lettuce than Jenny," said Greg.

"I don't like green food," said Jenny. "I like orange food like pumpkin pie."

"It's a good thing God gives us a rainbow of foods," said Grandma.

Think about your favorite foods. What green foods do you like? Can you think of orange-colored things that are good to eat?

Dear Jesus,

I like foods of different colors. I even like food that does not have much color at all like _____
_____. Thank You for giving me good things to eat. Amen.

What a rich harvest Your goodness provides!
Psalm 65:11

Rainbow Leftovers

Last time we talked about foods of different colors. Grandma mentioned that God gives us a rainbow of foods. At Jenny and Greg's house, there were so many leftovers from Thanksgiving that they had a rainbow meal. There was at least one food that started with each letter in the word *rainbow*. Finish their list.

R—rice

A—avocado dip and vegetables

I—ice cream with pumpkin pie

N— _____

B— _____

O— _____

W—Jenny and Greg couldn't think of a single food beginning with *W* on their after-Thanksgiving table. So they started their mealtime prayer with *W*. They began: "We thank You, God."

Now you finish talking to God.

Dear Jesus,
    I thank You, God, for _____
_____. Amen.

May all the peoples praise You.
Psalm 67:5

It Keeps Getting Better!

Everyone was almost ready to leave. The big Thanksgiving weekend was over. The relatives were all saying good-bye.

"I'll see you at Christmas," Tiffany said to her cousin Alan.

"You're lucky you still have Christmas," said Alan.

"Don't you have Christmas?" Tiffany asked.

"Oh, yeah," said Alan. "When you're older you still have a tree and presents, but Christmas is nicer when you're little."

Grandma had overheard the cousins talking. She put her arms around both of them. "I'll tell you a secret," Grandma said. "Every year gets better and better. This was the nicest Thanksgiving I ever had. Last year Tiffany's little sister wasn't even born. And this Christmas will be the best I ever had."

"Really, Grandma?" Tiffany asked.

"Sure," she said. "Last year we didn't have little Sarah. This year, she'll be our Christmas baby. Next year, she can learn about Jesus' birthday. And before long, she'll be able to read the story of the first Christmas."

"And I can tell her all about Christmas," said Tiffany. "I can't wait for this Christmas and next Christmas and next Christmas."

Dear Jesus,
    The older I get, the more I can learn about You. Amen.

He will take care of His flock like a shepherd.
Isaiah 40:11

Christmas Charades

Instructions: Act out the italicized words with your child.

Daddy was putting away the Thanksgiving decorations. At least, he was trying to. The children kept getting in the way.

"Kids, kids," he said. "Play a game. Act out a Christmas present you're going to give somebody."

"That's a neat game," said Whitney. *Pretend to play with them.*

Whitney *marched* around. Her *arms were straight* at her sides. She *stepped high*. She *opened and closed her mouth*.

"A nutcracker," guessed Kaitlyn.

"That's it," Whitney said. "I'm getting a nutcracker for Grandpa."

Kaitlyn *twirled around. Around and around.* That's all she did. The children couldn't guess the present.

"I'm a jewelry box with a dancer inside," she said. "Mommy and I are getting one for Chelsey. Don't tell her."

"Your turn, Daddy," the children said. "Your turn."

"Okay," he said. "Here's an easy one."

He didn't even get out of the chair. He just *sat*. He *held out his arms* and *pretended to rock a baby, back and forth, gently*.

"A baby," said Whitney. "We're going to have a baby!"

"No," smiled Daddy. "I was pretending to be Joseph, Jesus' father. Jesus is a gift for everybody."

Dear Jesus,

I'm thankful for the most important gift of all time—You. Amen.

Get the road ready for the Lord.
Mark 1:3

C'mon, Cousin

Alejandro was excited. His cousin was coming to visit!

Across the same city, Tricia was playing catch with her cousin, Emily.

Do you have a cousin? A cousin is a relative who sometimes lives near you. Other cousins don't know each other very well and live many miles apart.

What have you heard about cousins? Jesus had a cousin too. His name was John the Baptist. Jesus' cousin had a special job in life: John was supposed to tell people, "Look for my cousin."

But you know John said more than that. He said, "Look for Jesus. He will be your Savior."

Even for John, Jesus was more than a cousin. Jesus was John's Savior too.

Dear Jesus,

Sometimes I forget You were a person like I am, even having a cousin. I never forget, though, that You are my Savior. Amen.

The glory of the Lord is shining on you!
Isaiah 60:1

How Many Days Till?

"How many days until Christmas?" asked Courtney. How many days are there before you celebrate Christmas at your house?

"That's too long," said Courtney, hearing her mother's answer. "Christmas will never come."

"We're lucky," said Mother. "Think of the people who lived long ago, like it says in the Bible. They had to wait years before the first Christmas happened."

Then Courtney's mother had an idea. She cut some paper into strips.

"Every day until Christmas you can do something without being asked," said Mother. "You can pick up your toys, make a bed, give Skippy fresh water to drink, anything at all. Then I'll write it down on a slip of paper. We'll make a paper chain of ways you showed love around Christmas time."

Courtney wasn't so sure. It sounded like work. But counting down to Christmas started to be fun. Every day the chain grew longer. Courtney loved seeing Christmas come closer. And she felt good too, for another reason. Why do you think Courtney felt so good about the Christmas countdown?

Can you start a love chain at your house?

Dear Jesus,

Sometimes it seems like Christmas won't ever get here. Help me keep busy helping and showing what a good worker I can be. I can help by _____ _____. Amen.

*There will always be cold and heat,
summer and winter.*
Genesis 8:22

Winter Problems

Kaylee pulled and pulled. She couldn't tug her boot onto her foot. "Mommy, I need help," Kaylee called.

Then Kaylee yanked and yanked. The zipper wouldn't move on her warm winter coat. "Mommy, I need help," Kaylee called.

Finally she was ready for her mittens. The first mitten slid on smoothly. But where was the other? "Mommy, I hate winter," said Kaylee. "Now my mitten is lost."

Do you have any special winter problems? Sometimes it's hard getting used to dressing warmly for winter. Sometimes children are very hot by the time they are all ready to go outside.

But there are special things in winter. Winter is a special time of beauty. Can you draw a picture of a winter wonderland?

Dear Jesus,
    Winter is a hassle when _____
_____. But I like winter because _____
_____. Amen.

You can rest a while.
Mark 6:31

Take a Break

December can be a busy month. Where is one place you went yesterday? Where is somewhere you might go tomorrow?

It's good to relax, especially when there's so much happening.

Try some of these exercises: Breathe deeply, in and out, in and out. Now turn your head around. Now turn your head the other way. Let your arms flop down at your sides. Let your fingers hang heavy. Bring your shoulders up, then down, up, then down. Shake one foot and then the other.

It's good to relax, even when times are very busy.

Jesus took time to rest too. Tonight, before you go to bed, relax a bit. Then have a good night's sleep.

Dear Jesus,
    When I go to bed,
    I will rest my head.
    Then it's time to sleep,
    Rest, and dream so deep. Amen.

*This very day in David's town
your Savior was born.*
Luke 2:11

A Christmas Writer

"It's so long till Christmas," Angela complained.

"You're right, Angie," said Mother. "Christmas is still a few weeks away."

"I'm bored," said Angela. "What can I do?"

Her mother thought for a moment. Then she said, "Let's read about the first Christmas. Then you can write your own story about what happened."

Angela and her mother read Luke 2:4–14. Then Angie sat with a pencil and paper. Angela asked her mother how to spell some words. This is what she wrote.

The shepherds were watching their flocks at night,
When suddenly came a star so bright.
Then angels all around them played
And danced in a little parade.

Angela had written about the first Christmas. Then she drew a picture of baby Jesus with angels and shepherds. Can you draw about Christmas and write something too?

Dear Jesus,

My favorite thing about this time of year is _____
_____. Thank You for Christmas.
Amen.

They ... saw the Baby lying in the manger.
Luke 2:16

Let's Read

"Scoot over," said Catherine. "I want to sit on Mommy's lap."

"She's my mommy," said Grace.

"Well she's my mommy too," said Catherine.

"Girls, girls," said Mother. "Let's sit on the sofa so you can all see the pictures. I don't like to hear squabbling, especially when we're going to read the story of Christmas."

Have you read about Christmas yet this year? Which is your favorite Christmas book?

Dear Jesus,

I like to hear about when You were a baby. It makes me feel _____. I'm glad You are my Savior too. Amen.

Whoever loves is a child of God.
1 John 4:7

Knock, Knock

Instructions: Knock on a table every time the knocker bangs at Amy's house.

Knock, knock. Someone was at the door. It was the florist. Grandma had sent some pretty red flowers.

Knock, knock. Amy ran to the door. This time, maybe it would be for her! No, just a delivery. It was new boots for Daddy.

Knock, knock. Amy raced to the door. But no, it was the letter carrier with a big package for Mommy.

Knock, knock. Amy didn't run to the door. She sat on a chair with her head in her hands.

"What's wrong, honey?" asked Dad.

"There's no Christmas for me," Amy said sadly. "Christmas comes for everybody else."

"Oh, Amy," said Dad. "The deliveries have all been for others today. But Christmas comes for everybody. Jesus doesn't knock on our front door, but He comes into our hearts. He brings us the gift of love."

Amy's dad held her close. "If Jesus is in your heart, you can be glad other people get gifts," he said. "That's something you'll understand later, but just be glad, for now, that Jesus was born."

Dear Jesus,
    Sometimes I can be selfish like when _____
_____. One thing that's easy to share is the message of Christmas. I can do that by _____
_____. Amen.

She will have a son, and you will name Him Jesus.
Matthew 1:21

December Riddles

See if you can answer these December riddles.

A sign of love from the start,

For Valentine's Day but now too: a _____

_____. (*heart*)

Something that rings to tell,

"Jesus is born today": a _____

_____. (*bell*)

The doves in the stable coo,

"Jesus is born for me and _____

_____." (*you*)

What the Magi saw from afar

Shining over Bethlehem: a _____

_____. (*star*)

Dear Jesus,
 The signs of Christmas are around
 In stores and malls, cities, towns.
 Help me remember as I pray,
 What really counts on Christmas Day
 Is You are born, Christ Jesus, Lord.
 Your love, God's love, is what is heard.
 The wreaths and stars all shining bright
 Are just for You on Christmas night. Amen.

Jesus was born in the town of Bethlehem.
Matthew 2:1

Unpack Christmas

What a busy time it was at Kendra's house. Today was the day to unpack the Christmas boxes. Pretend to help Kendra. Open the first box. Look inside. Those are the Christmas lights. Now push that box aside for an adult to work with.

Here's another box—this one is heavy! Carefully unpack this box. What's inside your box?

Kendra still hasn't opened the box she really wants. Oh—now maybe this is it. Be careful holding the box! Yes, there's the picture on the side. There's a picture of Mary and Joseph and a baby. There's a picture of an angel and two shepherds. What box did Kendra find?

Each figure is wrapped in paper. Unroll the figures with Kendra. Where will you set up the créche at your house?

Dear Jesus,
When I see a manger set, I think of the first Christmas. You were just a baby. I know You grew up to be my Savior. Amen.

She gave birth to her first son.
Luke 2:7

Christmas in the Book

"Christmas is no fun anymore," said Kristin.

"Why, honey, it's not even Christmas Day yet," Mother said.

Kristin's mother was quiet for a moment. She thought of all the places they had shopped. Where have you gone Christmas shopping? She thought of what they had baked. Have you done Christmas baking? She thought of all the people they had wished a Merry Christmas. Whom have you said that to?

Then Kristin's mother said, "You're right, honey. We've forgotten what Christmas is all about."

"Where are you going, Mommy?" Kristin asked.

"To get Christmas," she answered. Her mother came back carrying a thick book. What book do you think she found? Can you find the story of Christmas in a Bible at your house?

Dear Jesus,

I know the story of the real Christmas is in the Bible. Help me remember that Christmas is really all about You. Amen.

I was a child.
1 Corinthians 13:11

Being Six

Shannon thought one of the best parts of celebrating Jesus' birthday was licking the Christmas cookie bowl. Ummm. The dough bits tasted good. Shannon's grandma watched her with a smile.

"You do that just like your mommy did," Grandma said.

"Mommy was never six years old," said Shannon.

"Oh, yes, she was," Grandma said. "And she loved to clean out cookie bowls at Christmas."

"Were you ever six years old, Grandma?" Shannon asked.

"My yes, honey," Grandmother said. "Everyone who grows up was once six years old."

"Even Uncle Billy was six, once?" Shannon asked.

Grandma nodded.

"Aunt Gladys?" Shannon asked.

Grandma nodded again.

"Even the Baby whose birth we're getting ready to celebrate was once six years old," Grandma said.

"It's hard to think of Jesus as a little boy," said Shannon. "I always think of Him grown up as my Savior."

How do you picture Jesus?

Dear Jesus,

It's exciting now, getting ready to celebrate Your birthday. When I think of You as a little boy, I _____
_____. When I think of You as my Savior, I want to say thank You. Amen.

Your deeds bring shouts of joy.
Psalm 65:8

Winter Sneaks Up

Instructions: Act out or make the sounds of the italicized words with your child.

Paige *shivered* under her coat. She had always lived where winters were just cool, not cold. Visiting Grandma up north in December was great, except for the weather.

"Let's *hurry up*, honey," said Grandma. "We've got just a bit more shopping to do."

"We've got a *roaring* winter ahead," said the clerk as they left the bakery.

"*Bundle up*," said the cashier at the card store. "Those winter temperatures will come *crashing* down tonight."

"Is winter always noisy here, Grandma?" Paige asked.

"The winds do *whistle*," said Grandma as they *walked* into the nice warm kitchen at home.

"And your grandma sure makes winter noisy when she *tromps* in with her boots on and *stomps* off the snow," teased Paige's grandfather with a smile.

That night in bed, Paige *listened* carefully. Would winter come *roaring* in during the night?

Suddenly, it seemed, it was time to wake up. Paige *tiptoed* cautiously to the window. She *gasped*. "Grandma," she called happily. "Winter *sneaked* in. It *snowed*!"

Dear Jesus,
Thank You for the surprises of the different seasons. In winter I especially like _____.
Amen.

It had been just as the angel had told them.
Luke 2:20

Where's Rudolph?

Daria loved to visit her friend's house at Christmastime. Mindy's house was a wonderland. Christmas decorations were everywhere Daria looked.

There was a candle plugged in at each window. Stockings were hung on the fireplace. There was a beautiful angel on top of the Christmas tree. Even the doorknobs were covered with little decorations.

Daria and Mindy wandered through the house, enjoying everything. But then Daria realized something was missing. "Where's Rudolph?" she asked. "You know, Santa's reindeer. And where is Santa Claus? I don't see a picture of him."

"Oh, we don't need that stuff," said Mindy. "We have Jesus."

The girls walked into the dining room. There on the table was a large manger set. The girls played with the figures all afternoon. When it was time for Daria to go home, she said, "You're right. I didn't miss Santa Claus at all at your house. Jesus fills up your Christmas."

How do you feel about that?

Dear Jesus,
Thank You for being born so we could have Christmas. Amen.

We should do good to everyone.
Galatians 6:10

Sharing Christmas

Delancey thought this was the best Christmastime ever. When his family bought a Christmas tree, they didn't buy one, they bought two. When they bought some new garland, they bought two boxes. When Delancey's mom mixed up the gingerbread for people to hang on the tree, his mom made a double batch.

This was going to be a great Christmas.

Delancey and his family would keep one of everything. The second tree, all decorated, would go to a family that wouldn't have had one.

Delancey was busy making ornaments. First he made an angel. What did the angels do at the first Christmas? Then he made a star. Why would a star be a good ornament? Next Delancey made a sheep. He covered this ornament with cotton balls. Why would a sheep be a good Christmas ornament? What ornament would you make?

Finally the tree was ready to be delivered.

"Oh, Daddy," Delancey whispered. "I'm so glad we can share Christmas."

Who will be a part of your Christmas celebration?

Dear Jesus,

One of the best things about Your birthday is _____ _____. Amen.

*Suddenly a great army of heaven's
angels appeared.*
Luke 2:13

The Angels Sing

Erica lay awake in bed. She was tired. The special church service had lasted very long. But she couldn't go to sleep. She kept remembering the play at church.

Erica loved wearing the garland on her head. She even felt like an angel standing by the manger. But poor James. Her baby brother had not been happy playing the part of baby Jesus. He cried and cried. And then when Erica and the other children started singing like angels, he really howled.

Erica loved the songs they had sung. She started humming softly. Now maybe she could get to sleep. But she heard something else. There was other singing. Was she dreaming about angels? No, the song was getting louder.

She crept downstairs. Her mom and dad were standing at the front door, looking out. Someone was outside.

"Mommy," Erica started to say.

"Why, honey, look who's here!" Mother said.

"I know," said Erica. "Real angels."

"No," Mother laughed. "These are some older children just singing like you did at church tonight. It is beautiful, though, isn't it?"

Erica nodded and crept back up the stairs. She wanted to fall asleep with the Christmas music still in her ears.

Now, sing one of your favorite Christmas songs that tells about the first Christmas.

Dear Jesus,
Thank You for the beautiful music of Your birth. Amen.

*This very day in David's town
your Savior was born.*
Luke 2:11

A Snowy Manger Scene

Brittany carefully unpacked the box. The mail carrier had brought a big heavy package. Brittany was happy to see all the presents inside. But something else was even more exciting—the Styrofoam packing pieces. She knew exactly how she was going to use them.

She collected all the little bits of white Styrofoam pieces from the floor. Then she took handful after handful to the créche under the Christmas tree.

Brittany stuck the Styrofoam snow under Mary's feet. She stuck snow under the manger. She even put a bit of snow on top of a donkey. Where would you add snow in your manger scene?

We know there wasn't any snow in Bethlehem at the first Christmas. But all over the world, children fix manger scenes in different ways. Some children dress the créche figures in bits of leftover fabric. Some children use foil to make a star to hang over the manger where Jesus lay. How do you make your créche special?

Dear Jesus,

Sometimes I like to rearrange the figures of our manger set. I like to tell the story of the first Christmas in my own words. But I know what is most important is that You were born. That's something that won't ever change. Amen.

Glory to God in the highest heaven.
Luke 2:14

Christmas Countdown

Can you count to 100? Can you count to 1,000? Let's count how many things and people were at the first Christmas.

There was one _____.

There might have been two _____.

There could have been three _____.

Perhaps there were four _____.

And there were lots of _____.

It's fun to play with numbers. But there's only one thing that really matters at Christmas: Jesus was born.

Dear Jesus,
On the first Christmas
There might have been 10 sheep,
There might have been 20 pigeons.
But You're the only Jesus,
And You were born for me.

On the first Christmas
There might have been two cows,
There might have been six geese.
But You're the only Jesus,
And You were born for me.
Thank You, Jesus. Amen.

I am here with good news for you.
Luke 2:10

What Shape Is Christmas?

"Children, please stay out of the kitchen," said Mrs. Kirby. "I need to finish wrapping these presents."

It was almost Christmas at the Kirby house. Elizabeth and Emily were excited! They kept getting in their mother's way.

"Take this paper and get some crayons and a pair of scissors," said Mrs. Kirby. "Go to your rooms and make an ornament for the tree in the shape of Christmas."

Elizabeth and Emily thought for a while. You think too. What shape is Christmas?

Elizabeth had an idea. She colored the paper green, then started cutting. She cut lots of pointed edges. What do you think Elizabeth made?

Emily finally had an idea too. She colored a big heart red.

"Oh, Emily," said Elizabeth. "Mommy said to make a shape for Christmas not Valentine's Day."

"But a heart is for Christmas," Emily said. "Love is what we feel in the air. You know, that warm feeling."

Can you make an ornament in the shape of Christmas?

Dear Jesus,
Thank You for Your love. Amen.

*Joseph went … to the town
of Bethlehem in Judea.*
Luke 2:4

A Picture-Perfect Christmas

Soo looked at the stack of Christmas cards. The top one showed two deer standing in snow, looking at the Baby in the manger. The card underneath had people walking to church through the snow. And Soo knew just what the other cards showed: snowy Christmas scenes.

Soo had never even seen snow, but it certainly looked beautiful. So clean, so soft. Then Soo got an idea.

He took a big bunch of white drawing paper from his room. Then he worked for a long time. What do you think he was doing?

"Soo, you've been quiet for a long time," said his mother, coming into the room. "Are you alr …?"

She looked around. The living room was covered with scraps of white paper. The sofa, the chairs, even the lower branches of the Christmas tree. Everything was covered with little bits of paper.

"We had a snowstorm," said Soo. "Now we can have a real Christmas like in the pictures."

His mother sat down on the snowy chair. "Soo," she said gently. "They probably didn't even have snow on the ground at the first Christmas."

Read about Jesus' birth. Is there anything said about snow?

Dear Jesus,
I know we don't need snow for Christmas. We just need You. Amen.

299

Don't be afraid.
Luke 2:10

A Nervous Angel

Brooke felt jittery. She was worried. What if she forgot her verse for the Christmas service? Brooke kept whispering the words to herself: "Fear not: for behold, I bring you good tidings of great joy, which shall be to all people."

It was almost her turn to talk. The shepherds were walking out. Now!

Brooke moved forward. She opened her mouth. She stopped. She couldn't remember what to say!

"Don't worry everybody. Jesus is born," she said. She moved back to be with the other angels. Oh, she had made a terrible mistake. She felt awful.

After church, she ran up to her father. "Oh, Daddy, I forgot what to say," Brooke cried.

"You were a great talking angel," said Dad. "You gave a wonderful message about Jesus. Remember what you said?"

"I told people not to worry because Jesus was born," Brooke said.

"That's the message of Christmas," Dad said. "Jesus was born to be our Savior. That's what Christmas is all about."

How do you think Brooke felt then?

Dear Jesus,

Help me remember the really important things about Christmas: _____. Amen.

My heart praises the Lord.
Luke 1:46

How Many Candles?

Jessica and Mack were busy in the kitchen. They were helping make a Jesus birthday cake. Act out what they were doing.

Crack two eggs.
Measure 1 cup sugar.
Sift 2 cups flour.
Add ½ stick butter.
Stir it all together.
Pour the batter into a pan.
Good job!

After the cake had baked, Jessica and Mack frosted it. But now there was a problem. How many candles should they put on Jesus' birthday cake? How many candles would you use?

"There shouldn't be any candles because we remember Jesus as just a baby at Christmastime," said Mack.

"There should be a whole bunch of candles because there have been so many Christmases," said Jessica.

How many candles would you put on Jesus' birthday cake?

Dear Jesus,
    Help me remember that You were born to be my Savior. Amen.

He has provided for us a mighty Savior.
Luke 1:69

What's Next?

We're going to play a Christmas word game. Turn to Luke 2 in a Bible. That will help you check the answers.

Mary and Joseph started to visit a town called Bethlehem. When they got there, what happened?

The shepherds were watching their sheep. An angel appeared. What happened then?

The shepherds watched the angels go away. What happened next?

You are so excited about Christmas. You know Jesus was born at Christmas. You want to tell others the Good News of Jesus. What will happen now?

Dear Jesus,

Christmas is a wonderful time to tell about You. Let me be a good helper for You, especially during these busy days. I can _____. Amen.

Let's go to Bethlehem.
Luke 2:15

Come and See!

Carrie hurried to get dressed. She knew just what she was going to make in the snow today.

Pretend to work with Carrie. First, start rolling some snow. Make a big ball. Now roll snow into a medium-size ball. Put it on top of the big ball. Now pat snow into a small ball. Stack it onto the other snowballs.

Now do the same thing again: a big ball, a medium ball, and a small ball on top. What will you add to make your snowball stacks look like people?

Carrie was getting cold. She ran into the house. "Come and see," she said to her father. "Look out the window."

"What nice snow people," Father said.

"Oh, no," said Carrie. "They're not just snow people. They're people coming to see baby Jesus."

And sure enough. It did look that way. Carrie had her snow people facing the cardboard manger figures on the front lawn.

Manger sets are everywhere so people can remember the first Christmas. Whom can you invite to church this Christmas to come and learn about Jesus?

Dear Jesus,

Some people don't know how You made Christmas happen. Help me remember to invite people to come to church with me. Amen.

The world and all that is in it belong to the Lord.
Psalm 24:1

Happy New Year!

It's almost the end of the year. Now is a good time to think back. Let's see what you can remember.

A place you visited: _____.

A person who helped you: _____.

An exciting thing that happened: _____.

A new person you met: _____.

Someone who loved you all year long: _____.

There were many good things about this last year. Good things are called blessings. There will be many good things about this next year. This next year will be a year of blessings. God promises that. God promises to bless you.

God also promises to love you. He promises to love you all year. Happy New Year!

Dear Jesus,
    Thank You for all the special blessings of this year: the people who loved me like
_____; the friends I played with like _____; the people I could love like _____.
Thank You for loving me. Amen.

Topical Index

Scripture Index